W9-AEK-179

rice

from risotto to sushi

rice

from risotto to sushi

Clare Ferguson

photography by Jeremy Hopley

RIZZOLI
NEW YORK

**My thanks in particular, to Ian Ferguson,
my husband, for his forbearance.**

Notes

Rice is best served immediately after cooking.
If it is to be served cold, or reheated, it should be
cooled quickly after cooking, covered, chilled quickly
in the coldest part of the refrigerator and then used
within 24 hours.
The herbs in this book are measured in bunches.
A large bunch consists of about 15 stems, and a small
bunch about 5 stems.
Rice has a subtle taste and requires assertive
seasoning with salt, chile, pepper, soy sauce, fish sauce,
or other salty-tasting agents, or sweet-sour flavors.

First published in the United States of America in 1997 by
RIZZOLI INTERNATIONAL PUBLICATIONS, INC.
300 Park Avenue South, New York, NY 10010

First published in Great Britain in 1997 by
Ryland Peters & Small
Cavendish House
51–55 Mortimer Street
London W1N 7TD

Text © Clare Ferguson 1997
Design and photographs © Ryland Peters & Small 1997

Art Director **Jacqui Small**
Art Editor **Penny Stock**
Editor **Elsa Petersen-Schepelern**
Photography **Jeremy Hopley**
Food Stylist **Clare Ferguson**
Stylist **Wei Tang**
Indexer **Hilary Bird**
Production **Kate Mackillop**

All rights reserved.
No part of this publication may be reproduced in any manner
whatsoever without permission in writing from Rizzoli
International Publications, Inc.

ISBN 0-8478-2000-9
LC 96-72030

Printed in Hong Kong

contents

Of the hundreds of different varieties of rice, some are used only in their country of origin, and others are widely used by cooks all over the world.

rice
varieties

Described on pages 140 and 141 are the **different** kinds of rice shown here, together with information about how to cook them and for how long, where to buy them, and how best to use them.

There are **numerous** categories: white, black, red, or brown in **color**; long, short, medium, or round in **shape**; glutinous (sticky) or not in **texture**; organic or not. Many rice varieties are also available in **easy-cook** form—misleading, because it actually takes longer to cook than ordinary rice. The process was first discovered in ancient India, where parboiling was used to preserve the rice and, in passing, also had the added advantage of forcing some of the nutrients, which are usually destroyed in milling, deep inside the grain.

The result is a food that is much more nutritionally valuable.

Glutinous red rice

White glutinous
Japanese sushi rice

Wild rice

White medium-grain
Calasparra paella rice

Red Camargue
wholegrain rice

White basmati rice

Brown basmati rice

Glutinous Thai
fragrant rice

Mixed basmati
and wild rice

Easy-cook
basmati rice

Brown long-grain
easy-cook rice

Wholegrain
long-grain rice

White round-grain
pudding rice

White medium-grain
Carnaroli risotto rice

White long-grain rice

long-grain white
easy-cook rice

Measuring Rice and Water

The easiest method is by volume: take one container of rice and add multiples of that container of hot water or stock; 1½ times for sushi rice, 2 for most other kinds of rice, 3 for risotto, or 4 for paella. Bring to a boil, cover the pan, reduce the heat, simmer until done—usually, though not always, for 12 minutes. This method, translated into ounces and cups, is used in this book. Alternatively, for boiled rice, cover the rice with liquid to a depth of one finger joint above the rice. Boil, cover, reduce the heat, simmer till done (usually 12 minutes). A Malaysian friend taught me this method when we were students together. It works!

how to
cook rice

The best methods for cooking rice range from the most traditional to the most up-to-date and high-tech!

Washing Rice

Asian cooks routinely wash rice before cooking, and sometimes soak it too. I do not believe this is necessary with rice produced by modern farming and milling methods.

Absorption Method

Cover rice with boiling liquid, return to a boil, uncovered. Cover, reduce immediately to the lowest possible heat. Avoid lifting the lid. After 10, 12, 15, or 25 minutes, as listed in the recipes (depending on rice type), it will be cooked and all liquid absorbed. Steam holes may appear on the surface. Turn heat off. Let stand (foil covered, cloth wrapped, or not) for a few minutes to allow the grains to fluff up and lighten—or serve straight away.

Pan-of-Water Method

Measure rice into a large pan. Add copious boiling water or stock. Do not cover. Bring back to a boil, reduce to a medium simmer and cook 10, 12, 15, 25, or more minutes, appropriate to the rice type or until tender. Turn off the heat and strain through a sieve. Return rice to the pan, or to a colander set over the still-hot pan. Let stand for a few minutes, then serve.

Electric Rice Cooker

These convenient, fool-proof machines make cooking rice child's play. You should follow the instructions given with each machine, but the usual method is to measure the rice, then add the level of water relevant to that type. Add no salt. Cover and switch on. When rice is done, the machine turns off automatically and the rice will keep hot for up to 1 hour. (After that it will begin to deteriorate.) It's perfect for families who eat at different times, though some cooks think this method is somewhat impersonal. Glutinous rice can also be cooked this way, though it takes longer—a microwave is a good alternative.

Cooking Rice in a Microwave

Though no faster than conventional methods it is effortless and useful since the machine automatically turns off and residual heat warms and fluffs up the rice. Choose a large, medium height, non-metal microwaveable casserole or covered bowl. Add 1 scoop (e.g. 1 cup) rice. Measure in 1¾ scoops of liquid for sushi rice, 2 for white or brown rice, 3 for Camargue and Thai red rice, wild rice, or risotto rice, and 4 for Calasparra or Bomba rice. Cover. For all kinds of rice, in 750 watt models, microwave on HIGH/FULL POWER for 10 minutes or until boiling. Then, for white rice, reduce to MEDIUM/50% POWER for 10–12 minutes. Let stand undisturbed for 5 minutes. For wild, brown, and Camargue red rice, reduce to MEDIUM/50% POWER, cook 30 minutes, let stand 5 minutes. For Thai red rice, reduce to MEDIUM/50% POWER, cook 20 minutes, let stand for 5 minutes. Easy-cook rice of any variety will take 3–4 minutes longer at MEDIUM/50% POWER than the untreated form of that variety. To reheat previously cooked rice, cover and microwave on HIGH/FULL POWER for 3–4 minutes (or 6–8 minutes for wild or brown rice).

Note: *These timings are for a 750 watt model. If yours is of higher wattage, deduct 10 seconds per minute of the recipe for every 100 watts. If lower, add 10 seconds per minute of the recipe for each 100 watts.*

Cooking in a Pressure Cooker

Useful for brown rice. Specific instructions should be followed for each model, but this is the general method. Leave the low trivet in position. Add the measured rice. Cover with boiling water or stock. Set the lid in position, bring to a gentle simmer, turn the pressure gauge to the higher pressure, reduce the heat, and leave to cook. Turn off and remove the pan from the heat. Allow the steam vent to reduce its plume of steam, then let the pan and its contents cool enough to let the pressure reduce. Uncover.

Cooking Rice in the Oven

This is a good but rather slow method. Perhaps the most famous dish cooked in this way is the traditional English rice pudding, where rice, sugar, eggs, and milk are cooked in a moderate oven for about 50 minutes.

Steamed Rice

When Asian cooks or restaurants specify "steamed rice", they may well mean rice cooked in boiling water and steam by the absorption method or even in an electric rice cooker. Traditional South-east Asian recipes for steamed sticky rice may need specific methods relevant to these cultures, where rice cooking is taken to a high art. Follow the recipe instructions, or adapt the method to the utensils you have available.

Sake

(*Japanese rice wine*)

Pale to deep gold. Sherry, diluted gin or vodka, dry vermouth, or Chinese rice wine can be substituted. *Cooking and timing:* Use in batters, marinades, dressings, sauces. To serve as a beverage, heat gently over hot water, but do not overheat, or the alcohol will be driven off. Refrigerate any leftover sake after opening.

Mirin

(*Japanese sweetened rice wine*)

Clear pale yellow liquid, more diluted than sake. If unavailable, substitute as for sake.

Cooking and timing: Used in cooked rice, dressings.

Rice Vinegar

(*Red, Clear white, Yellow or Black rice vinegar*)

Used in dressings, marinades, sauces, dips, and rice dishes. Red is mellow, fruity, (almost like balsamic vinegar) with decisive flavor. Clear white is sharp, yellow is mellow, black tastes caramelized. Japanese white rice vinegar is milder than Chinese.

Rice Vermicelli Noodles, Rice Sticks or Wide Rice Sticks

(*Vietnamese soup noodles, bañh pho*)

Dry, translucent, rice-flour pasta, looped into skeins. Range from very fine vermicelli to wide rice sticks about ½ inch across. Disregard package cooking instructions which are rarely accurate.

Cooking and timing: Rehydrate in hand-hot or near-boiling water for 5–15 minutes (traditional method is a long soak in cold water). Drain and serve as is, or reheat. Steam-heat, poach, quickly stir-fry, deep-fry, or add to composite dishes.

Vietnamese Ricepaper Wrappers

(*Rice wrappers, bañh trang*)

Dried 8- or 10-inch ricepaper circles or segments. Eaten raw, steamed, or wrapped around fillings, they must first be moistened by dipping in water, brushing or spraying with water.

Deep-fried, they can also be served as crisps.

Cooking and timing: Soften in hand-hot water, then prepare as above.

other rice products

Ricepaper Wrappers

Wide Rice Sticks

Yellow Rice Vinegar

White Rice Vinegar

Red Rice Vinegar

Rice Sticks

Ricepaper

Japanese *Harusame* Noodles

("Spring Rain" noodles, fine rice noodles)
Dried hair-thin filaments, virtually translucent, made of rice flour (some are also made from potato or tapioca flour). Sold in skeins.
Cooking and timing: As for rice vermicelli noodles.

Mochi Rice Cakes

Hard, dry, dense blocks of pounded, cooked glutinous rice. Not to be confused with fresh *mochi* cakes which are a ready-to-eat snack.
Cooking and timing: Soften and rehydrate by soaking for 5 to 15 minutes in very hot water. Drain then grill or poach. Use in composite dishes such as soups or casseroles.

Ground Rice

Coarse to medium ground meal. Used to make desserts, batters, milk puddings, crisp doughs. Useful thickener, but glutinous rice flour better for fine biscuits, doughs, batters, wrappers.
Cooking and timing: Generally 2 oz. added to 2½ cups of hot liquid. Cooks in 10 to 15 minutes.

Rice Flour

Fine flour used for thickening, and to give lightness to sauces, batters, and doughs, such as in the steamed buns and *dim sum* of China and Southeast Asia. Also used in Asian pasta making. Inexpensive and convenient.
Cooking and timing: Used in doughs, mixtures.

Flaked Rice

Used for puddings, cereals, quick cooking, and thickening in hot liquid.
Cooking and timing: 2 oz. cooked 10 to 12 minutes in 2½ cups hot milk, until thick and creamy.

Rice Cakes

Proprietary snack food, low-calorie, gluten-free. Used with or without toppings as a diet food.

Ricepaper

Made from the fibers of 2 or 3 rice-like plants. Used under baked items to prevent sticking, but is edible, even without cooking. When baking, use moderate oven heat. Brittle when dry.

Ground Rice

Rice Cakes

Harusame Noodles

Mochi Rice Cakes

Flaked Rice

Rice Flour

Rice Vermicelli Noodles

the
americas

Wild rice is the only rice native to North America. However, the many waves of **migration** to the New World has resulted in great, classic rice dishes, that utilize all the other kinds of rice. Dishes range from **gumbo** and **jambalaya** to the creations of modern chefs.

lobster and lemon risotto

on a bed of bitter greens

A superbly luxurious taste of the sea: freshly cooked lobster nestling on lemony risotto and a bed of fresh-tasting salad herbs for contrast. If live lobsters are unappealing or unavailable, buy a recently cooked one and proceed with the recipe the same way, using either ready-made fresh fish stock or fish stock cubes to help boost the flavor of the broth. The dried Japanese-style *wakame* "sea vegetable" helps add to the sea-savor. Buy *wakame* from a Japanese grocer, specialist deli, or wholefood store and use the best risotto rice you can afford. Cheese is an entirely optional addition.

2 tablespoons extra-virgin olive oil

4 tablespoons butter

2 leeks, white parts only, finely sliced

2 cups white Italian risotto rice
(such as *superfino* grade of Carnaroli,
Arborio, Roma, or Boldo, or *semifino*
grade of Vialone nano or Padano)

⅔ cup dry white wine, such as
sauvignon blanc

5 cups hot lobster and fish stock
(see below), or fish stock

1 lemon

2 oz. finely shredded Parmesan cheese
(optional)

8 oz. mixed bitter greens, such as
cress, rocket, mizuna, endive, and
dandelion, to serve

½ teaspoon mild paprika, to serve

Fish Stock:

3 tablespoons sea salt

1 oz. dried *wakame* seaweed (if available)

1 small, live lobster, about 1½ lb.,
or a ready-cooked lobster

1 teaspoon white peppercorns, crushed

1 head of fennel, quartered,
or 3 celery stalks

12 parsley stalks

1 lb. bones and trimmings from white
fish such as turbot or cod

Serves 4

To make the fish stock, bring a large pan of water to a boil, together with 3 tablespoons sea salt and the seaweed, if using: there should be enough water to cover the lobster by 2 inches. If using a live lobster plunge it into the boiling water, return to a boil and cook at a rolling boil for 12 minutes, until the lobster turns completely red. Remove the lobster, drain it well, reserving the cooking liquids, and cool over ice for about 10 to 15 minutes.

Crack open the claws and extract the meat. Cut open the body and tail and remove the edible meat in pieces as large as possible. Discard the inedible parts. Cut the tail meat into thick slices.

Crush the thorax and all the remaining debris and put in a clean pan. Add 3 cups of the strained cooking liquid, 2½ cups cold water, the peppercorns, fennel or celery, parsley stalks, and the fish bones and trimmings. Bring to a boil, cover, and simmer for about 10 minutes. Strain, taste, and adjust the seasoning. Measure 4 cups of this stock into a pan, then reheat and keep hot.

To make the risotto, heat the oil and half the butter in a medium heavy-bottom saucepan. Add the leeks and sauté gently for 1 to 2 minutes. Add the rice, stir until well coated, then add the wine. Let it bubble.

Add a quarter of the hot stock and stir gently. Cook over a gentle heat for about 6 to 7 minutes, stirring now and then, until the liquid is absorbed. Continue to add the stock 3 or 4 times more until it is all used. The risotto should be tender, but rich, moist, and glossy.

Cut the zest from the lemon into 4 long strips, curl the strips into twists, and set aside. Squeeze the juice from the lemon.

Add the remaining butter to the risotto, followed by lemon juice to taste, and finely shredded Parmesan, if using. Stir, cover, and allow to heat through.

To serve, put a tangle of salad leaves on each plate and spoon the risotto on top. Put the lobster meat on top of the risotto, sprinkle with paprika, add a twist of lemon zest, and serve hot.

pan-fried crab cakes
with spicy oriental sauce

This dish is a blend of several great recipes I first tasted in Louisiana and San Francisco. If no fresh crabmeat is available, use defrosted crab. If you have only cooked crab, mix it half and half with raw, minced white fish: it is the dense texture of raw seafood that defines this dish. Season well: the mild sweetness makes salting important.

Put the rice in a medium saucepan with the boiling stock. Return to a boil, cover the pan, and reduce the heat to very low. Leave undisturbed for about 18 minutes or until the grains are tender and plump, and all the liquid is absorbed. Put the pan in a bowl of iced water to cool the rice.

To prepare the crab cakes, finely slice the green tops of the scallions lengthwise. Pour boiling water over them, drain, and refresh in cold water. Set aside. Chop the white parts finely. Pick over the crabmeat and discard any shell or debris. Put the crab in a food processor together with the chopped white scallions, ground rice, egg, salt, and five-spice. Process in short bursts to amalgamate. (If using cooked crab and raw fish, process these together for a minute or so, in brief bursts, before adding the other ingredients.)

Stir 2½ cups of cooked rice into the food processor. Process in brief bursts until amalgamated. Do not over-process. Divide the mixture into patties—eight 3-inch diameter as a main course, or eighteen 1½-inch as an appetizer. Heat half the oil in a heavy-bottom, preferably nonstick skillet. Cook 4 patties at a time, for 2 minutes each side. Keep hot. Combine all the sauce ingredients in a small bowl or pitcher. Mix the scallion greens into the remaining rice. Serve the rice topped with the crab cakes and the sauce spooned over.

2 cups easy-cook basmati-wild-rice-mix

3 cups hot chicken stock

6 scallions

1 lb. prepared raw crabmeat,
or 6 oz. cooked crabmeat mixed
with 6 oz. raw minced white fish

1 oz. ground rice

1 egg

1–2 teaspoons salt

2 teaspoons Chinese five-spice powder

1–2 tablespoons virgin olive oil,
for cooking

salad greens, to serve (optional)

Spicy Oriental Sauce:

3 tablespoons oyster sauce

3 tablespoons hoisin sauce

1 tablespoon light soy sauce

2 tablespoons sweet ginger wine, or
other dessert wine

1 teaspoon Tabasco sauce

Serves 4 as main course, 6 as appetizer

red mullet tamales

with tomato chile dip

Tamales are usually made from corn, but these also contain ground rice. If there is no fresh corn with green husks available, use dried husks from Spanish or Mexican food shops, and rehydrate them in warm water. Chiles, polenta, and *masa harina*, the lime-treated corn flour used in tortillas, are found in the same shops. You can also use frozen green corn husks, and frozen or canned corn "niblets", mashed a bit with a potato masher. Three corn cobs should yield about 8 oz., enough for 6 appetizers.

12 oz. fish fillets, such as red mullet, snapper, gurnard, bream, or bass
juice of 3–4 limes
1 green jalapeño chile, finely sliced lengthwise
3 fresh corn cobs, including the green husks
1 cup rice flour
⅓ cup fine polenta (cornmeal)
⅓ cup *masa harina* (limed corn flour)
½ teaspoon chile powder
1 teaspoon salt
1 tablespoon snipped fresh oregano or marjoram leaves
1 egg, beaten
½ oz. dried chile, such as ancho or chipotle, crumbled or chopped
3 ripe red tomatoes, finely diced
salt, to taste
Serves 6 as an appetizer

tamales de pescado

1 Cut the fish into 24 equal pieces and put them into a non-reactive dish. Add the lime juice and the jalapeño chile. Stir well and set aside to marinate while the tamale dough is prepared.

2 Remove the green husks from the corn and put them in a bowl of hot water. Discard the silk. Using a coarse grater, grate the fresh corn to a pulp. Discard the central cores. (There should be about 8 oz. of pulp.)

3 Mix the pulp with the rice flour, polenta, *masa harina*, chile powder, salt, and herbs. Add the beaten egg and 2 or 3 tablespoons of fish marinade. Mix to a soft, pliable, putty-like dough. Drain the fish and reserve the marinade.

4 Drain the husks. Put a piece of fish at the end of a husk, with a heaped tablespoon of dough on top. Wrap up loosely, over and over, until half enclosed. With a second husk, wrap at right angles. Secure with string or skewer.

5 Repeat with all the remaining tamales. Steam over rapidly boiling water for 15 to 20 minutes, turning the parcels after 10 minutes. Test by unwrapping: the fish should be white and the dough firm.

6 Simmer the reserved marinade for 4 minutes, then add the crumbled dried chile. Add the diced tomato and stir. Serve with the tamales.

Note: If you don't have enough corn husks, use oiled foil strips instead.

RED MULLET TAMALES 21

jambalaya

traditional jambalaya
with chorizo and shrimp

The word "jambalaya" is Louisiana Creole: *jam* is from *jambon*, the French word for ham, *à la* means "of" or "with", and *ya* is an old African word for rice. Jambalaya relates to Senegalese *tiebe* dishes, Caribbean pilaus, and Spanish paella. It includes the Southern culinary "trinity" of celery, green bell pepper, and onion, and a brown roux of butter and flour, a pivotal element in Southern cooking.

Heat the oil in a large, heavy-bottom, flameproof casserole dish. Stir in the flour, if using, and cook to a golden-brown roux. Add the pork and sausage. Cook, stirring and turning, for 6 to 7 minutes until brown. Remove from the pan with a slotted spoon. Add the chicken and sauté until golden-brown and firm. Return the pork and sausage to the pan, add the celery, onion, garlic, bell pepper or chiles, bouquet garni, and chile flakes. Stir for 2 minutes more. Add the tomatoes and rice, and stir until the rice is well coated. Add the hot stock, return to a boil, cover, and reduce to a gentle simmer. Cook undisturbed for 10 to 12 minutes, then add the ham and shrimp. Cover and cook for another 4 to 5 minutes until the shrimp are pink and firm, the ham hot, the liquid almost completely absorbed, and the chunks of meat plump and tender. Stir gently. Cover the pan and stand for 3 to 4 minutes with the heat turned off. Serve from the casserole.

3 tablespoons canola or corn oil

2 tablespoons all-purpose flour (optional)

12 oz. pork shoulder, boneless pork chops, or fillet, cut into 1-inch chunks

12 oz. spicy pork link sausage, (chorizo or *andouille*), cut into 1-inch chunks

8 boneless, skinless chicken thighs

2 celery stalks, sliced

1 large onion, sliced

4 garlic cloves, crushed

1 green bell pepper, seeded, cored, and diced, or 2 seeded jalapeño chiles

1 bouquet garni (a bundle of fresh bay, thyme, parsley, and sage, tied together)

1 teaspoon dried chile flakes

1 lb. ripe fleshy red tomatoes, chopped

2½ cups white long-grain rice

4 cups boiling chicken or pork stock

4 oz. smoked ham, in long slices

8 oz. uncooked shrimp, shell-on

salt and freshly ground black pepper

Serves 4–6

cajun gumbo
with Jerusalem artichokes

Gumbo has an intriguing and exotic past with French, Spanish, and African heritage. It evolved out of necessity but it has been elevated to the glorious. *Gombo* is French for "okra". Traditionally okra is trimmed to show its interior and oozes sticky juices which enrich the texture of the dish. I prefer to trim just a little from the stem end, without exposing the interior, so it cooks tender but firm. Filé powder, a traditional thickener and flavoring made from sassafras trees, is available from specialist shops.

2 tablespoons fruity olive oil

8 oz. chorizo, **Cajun**, or **Creole** spicy sausage, or boudin, cut in chunks

6 chicken thighs

2 onions, quartered

4 celery stalks, with leaves reserved, then scissor-snipped

2 green bell peppers, halved, seeded, and cubed

1 big bunch of fresh thyme

2 hot chiles, such as jalapeño or serrano, seeded and chopped

1 teaspoon allspice berries, crushed

2 teaspoons white peppercorns, crushed

8 oz. Jerusalem artichokes, scrubbed and thinly sliced

2½ cups spicy stock, such as pork

2 tablespoons filé powder (or extra thyme leaves plus 2 tablespoons arrowroot for thickening)

about 13 oz. canned red kidney beans, in chile sauce

1–2 teaspoons Tabasco sauce

1 cup plus 1 tablespoon white easy-cook long-grain rice, such as Carolina

4 oz. okra, tops minimally trimmed

2 plum tomatoes, diced

Serves 4–6

1 Heat the olive oil in a large, heavy-bottom flameproof pan. Add the thick chunks of spicy sausage, the chicken thighs, and the quartered onions, then sauté for 6 to 8 minutes until lightly browned.

2 Thickly slice the celery stalks (but not the leaves) and add to the pan together with the green bell pepper, thyme, chiles, crushed allspice berries, and crushed peppercorns. Sauté for a further 5 minutes.

3 Add the thinly sliced artichokes, together with the hot spicy stock, then return to a boil, cover the pan with a lid, reduce the heat, and simmer gently for another 20 minutes. Mix the filé powder with a little water.

4 Stir in the canned beans and their chile sauce, Tabasco to taste, and the green filé mixture. Heat through until thickened slightly. Wash and drain the rice and put in a shallow saucepan. Add double its volume of boiling water.

5 Bring the rice back to a boil, cover, reduce the heat, and simmer for about 15 minutes. Add the trimmed okra after 8 minutes: it will cook in the steam. Let stand 3 minutes.

6 Serve the gumbo with the rice, in generous bowls, garnished with the reserved celery leaves and diced tomato. Alternatively, serve the gumbo first, then serve the rice afterwards, to stir into the juicy gravy.

Modern Florida cooking is very adventurous: passionfruit and lime are used to marinate the fish, and then added to the dressing. Wild rice is native to America, and makes a delicious, modern salsa when mixed with black beans and the spicy, fruity marinade.

seared swordfish
with wild rice and black bean salsa

4 swordfish steaks, about 6 oz. each, cut about ½ inch thick

6 garlic cloves, cut into 5 or 6 slivers

salt and freshly ground black pepper

Black Bean Salsa:

¾ cup dried small black soybeans, turtle beans, or kidney beans (or 14 oz. canned black kidney beans)

1 onion, quartered

1 bouquet garni or bunch of thyme

1 cup wild rice

6 tablespoons chopped fresh cilantro

2 scallions, chopped

2 hot chiles, seeded and chopped

Passionfruit and Lime Marinade:

1 teaspoon sea salt

pulp or juice of 6 passionfruit

1 teaspoon cumin seeds, crushed

2 red bell peppers, seeded and diced

⅔ cup extra-virgin olive oil

1 teaspoon peppercorns, crushed

juice of 6 limes

Serves 4–6

To make the salsa, first soak the dried beans overnight in cold water to cover. Next day, drain the soaked beans and add enough boiling water to cover the beans by 3 inches. Add the onion and bouquet garni. Bring to a boil, then simmer part-covered for 1¼ to 1½ hours until the beans are soft enough to squash easily between the fingers. After 45 minutes, put the wild rice in a pan with 4 cups boiling water. Return to a boil, cover, and simmer for 40 to 45 minutes until the grains are tender and some are splitting at the ends. Let stand for about 10 minutes, then drain.

Make 8 cuts in each fish steak, 4 on each side, and insert slivers of garlic. To make the marinade, mix the salt, passionfruit, cumin, red bell pepper, oil, pepper, and half the lime juice. Beat briefly. When the rice is half cooked, pour the mixture over the fish. Leave to marinate for 20 minutes. Reserve about 6 tablespoons of the beans and put the remainder in a bowl with the rice.

Boil the marinade in a pan for 1 minute. Add the remaining lime juice. Pour half this mixture into a bowl, and stir the remainder through the rice and beans.

To finish the salsa, add the cilantro, scallions, chiles, and reserved beans to the bowl of marinade. Season generously. Season the fish, then cook on a preheated broiler, barbecue, or stove-top grill pan for 2½ to 3 minutes: no longer or it will dry out. Set the fish on the rice-bean base, add the salsa, and serve hot, warm, or cool, but not chilled.

rice and peas
with Jamaican hot chile sauce

Peas or beans with rice is one of the world's greatest food combinations. Depending on the culture and location, "peas" could mean pigeon peas, black-eyed peas, gunga, gungo, goongo, or Congo peas, red beans, black beans, or even fava beans. Refer to a specialist cookbook for the different soaking and cooking times needed for each variety—kidney beans, for example, must be thoroughly boiled to eliminate toxins. In this recipe, hot Caribbean chiles are left whole but pierced, to provide fruitiness as well as heat.

2½ cups dried peas or beans, such as pigeon peas, gungo, black-eyed peas, red or black kidney beans, or black turtle beans*

2 habanero or Scotch bonnet chiles, pierced several times with a needle

1 onion, quartered

1½ lb. smoked shoulder bacon or ham, or 1 bacon or ham hock

2½ cups white long-grain rice, or white easy-cook rice

1¾ cups canned coconut milk

Chile Sauce:

4 garlic cloves

2 medium hot green chiles, such as serrano or jalapeño

1 bunch of fresh oregano

1 bunch of fresh flat-leaf parsley

8 scallions, chopped

juice of 5 limes or 3 lemons

1 tablespoon mixed French mustard

salt, to taste

Serves 6–8

*Dried peas or beans should be soaked overnight, then cooked, according to their variety, as described in Step 6.

1 To soak the peas or beans, cover with cold water, and leave overnight, or pour over boiling water, cover with a lid, and soak for 1 hour. Drain. If using red beans, soak, then boil vigorously for 15 minutes and discard the water.

2 Put the beans in a pan with boiling water to cover by 3 inches. Add the chiles, onion, and bacon, ham, or pork. Boil for 10 minutes, part-cover, and cook at a moderate boil according to the times in Step 6, or until fairly tender.

3 Add rice and coconut milk. Simmer, part-covered, 16 to 18 minutes. Drain off any liquid into a pan, reduce to 2 tablespoons, and return to the beans. Discard the chiles. Remove the meat, chop into pieces, then return to the pan.

4 To make the chile sauce, crush the garlic, seed and slice the chiles, and snip the herbs. Put with the other sauce ingredients in a food processor. Whizz for the minimum time it takes to form a sauce.

5 Carefully remove the cooked habanero or Scotch bonnet chiles from the pan, and discard. Serve the rice and peas in bowls with a dollop of chile sauce on top, and serve the remaining sauce separately.

6 Cooking times for presoaked peas or beans are 40 to 50 minutes for red or black kidney beans, 1¼ to 1½ hours for black-eyed and gungo peas, 1½ to 2 hours for black turtle beans.

Many European rice dishes are a legacy of that continent's **colonial** past, especially **kedgeree**, Britain's favorite dish from the great days of the Raj. Spain and Italy, however, have created their own classic rice dishes, **paella** and **risotto**, using local strains of rice.

europe

Kedgeree, that remnant of Britain's Indian colonial past, depends on first-class ingredients and recently cooked, cool (not chilled, not hot) rice for its full charm. Though traditionally a breakfast dish, it is perfect for brunch, lunch, or a late, informal supper meal. If you have other smoked seafood such as scallops, mussels, oysters, or even clams, these too may be added to the poaching water to reheat before mixing with the rice. Versatile, elegant, easy, and utterly delicious, especially when accompanied by a cold, crisp sauvignon blanc or champagne.

kedgeree
with smoked fish and crème fraîche

I lb. smoked haddock
½ stick unsalted butter
2 medium red onions, finely sliced
3–4 garlic cloves, chopped
I teaspoon coriander seeds, crushed
I pinch of turmeric or saffron
8 oz. cooked white basmati rice
2 soft-boiled (4 minutes) eggs
½ cup crème fraîche
I medium hot red chile, seeded, blanched, and finely sliced (optional)
sea salt and freshly ground pepper
sprigs of parsley, to serve
Serves 4

Poach the fish in a little water for 4 to 6 minutes until it flakes easily. Discard the skin, remove any bones, break the fish into chunky pieces, then return it to its still-hot cooking liquid. If you plan to use any other cooked seafood, add it to the cooking liquid at this time.

Heat the butter in a pan and add the onions, garlic, coriander seeds, and turmeric or saffron, and sauté for 2 minutes. Add the drained, flaked fish, the cooked rice, I to 2 tablespoons of poaching liquid, and the eggs, shelled and cut into quarters. Cover the pan and reheat for 2 minutes. Stir in the salt and freshly ground black pepper, the crème fraîche, and sliced red chile, if using.

Pile into a serving dish, add sprigs of parsley, and serve hot. Triangles of fresh hot toast make a pleasant accompaniment.

Suppli are rice balls, cooked to pleasing crispness outside, melted and gooey inside. The dribbly melted mozzarella cheese oozes strings or "wires", the origin of their charming Italian name. Use risotto left over from an earlier meal—cook extra because *suppli* are so delicious—or other cooked round-grain rice. The key thing is to ensure that the rice, at the outset, is flavorful: under-seasoned *suppli* are disappointing.

supplì al telefono

suppli cheese balls
with basil and pignoli nuts

½ cup pignoli nuts

2 lb. seasoned, cooked risotto rice

2 medium eggs, beaten

1 bunch of basil, finely sliced

3 oz. Parma ham, thinly sliced, cut into 36 squares

4 oz. buffalo mozzarella, cut into 36 little strips

1 cup dry breadcrumbs

olive oil, for frying

Makes about 36, serves 6–8

Preheat the broiler, line the broil pan with foil, and toast the pignoli nuts, shaking them occasionally under the heat until they are evenly golden brown. Fold these into the rice, together with the eggs and basil. Mix well.

Shape, using clean hands, into about 36 walnut-sized balls. Use your index finger to push a hole into the center of each. Insert a piece of ham, followed by a piece of mozzarella. Pinch closed and squeeze the ball back into shape.

Roll each cheese ball in breadcrumbs, then chill.

Heat the oil in a deep-fryer or saucepan to 375°F or until a cube of bread turns golden brown in 40 seconds. Using a frying basket, cook several at a time, rolling them around and turning them over with tongs, so that the *suppli* are evenly golden brown all over (about 3 minutes). Be sure there is enough oil to cover the *suppli*, or they may split during cooking because of uneven expansion.

Drain on crumpled paper towels and keep hot until all the *suppli* are cooked.

Serve hot as an appetizer, or as party food.

caldo verde soup

A classic Portuguese soup—hot, spicy, and outstandingly delicious. It depends upon fresh greens, good broth, garlic, chile, potatoes and, in this version, rice too. A marvelously adaptable recipe that varies from this thick, hearty form to clear broths with a few shreds of potato and greens.

Heat the oil or fat in a large heavy-bottom pan and add the onions, garlic, chile, rice, and potatoes. Sauté 2 to 3 minutes. Chop the parsley and cilantro and reserve half of each. Add the remainder to the pan, followed by the cabbage and the greens. Pour in the pork stock and season to taste.

Bring the soup to a boil, cover, and simmer for about 20 to 25 minutes, or until pulpy and tender. Pour through a colander or strainer, reserving the liquid and solids but discarding the chile. Put the reserved parsley and cilantro in a blender or food processor, add about one-third of the liquid and solids, and blend to a purée. Return the purée and the remaining soup to the pan and return to a boil. Taste and adjust the seasoning.

Meanwhile, if using bacon, cut it into lardons (matchstick strips) or, if using pancetta, cut it into cubes. Put the lardons or cubes into a small pan and sauté in their own fat until crisp. Pour the pan contents into the soup. Heat the caraway seeds in a second pan until aromatic, sprinkle over the soup, and serve, accompanied by some crusty country bread.

3 tablespoons good virgin olive oil, lard, or bacon fat

2 onions, quartered and sliced

4 garlic cloves, crushed

I hot green chile, such as serrano, slit open lengthwise

½ cup long-grain rice

6 oz. potatoes, cut in ½-inch cubes

I large bunch of fresh flat-leaf parsley

2 large bunches of fresh cilantro

8 oz. dark green cabbage, such as Savoy

4 oz. Swiss chard, spinach, beet greens, or broccoli tops

6 cups flavorful pork stock

2 oz. bacon or pancetta

I–2 teaspoons caraway seeds

sea salt and freshly ground black pepper

Serves 4–6

A glorious, sunshine-colored Provençal soup, using the dry, brilliantly orange-fleshed pumpkin (*calabaza*, in West Indian markets), with its dark, heavy rind, firm flesh, and hard seeds. You could substitute a firm, dense squash, such as Hubbard or butternut, but not watery summer squash.

soupe de potiron

pumpkin chowder
with rice and thyme

2½ lb. orange-fleshed pumpkin, peeled and seeded

I large Spanish onion, sliced

2½ cups well seasoned chicken stock

I teaspoon dried crushed chiles

1½ teaspoons salt

I cinnamon stick, broken

I small bunch of thyme, plus extra to serve

I fresh bay leaf, bruised

½ cup white long-grain rice

1¼ cups whole milk

Serves 6

Cube the pumpkin and put in a pan with the onion, stock, chiles, salt, cinnamon, thyme, and bay leaf. Bring to a boil, cover, and cook for 20 minutes or until done. Meanwhile, put the rice in another pan with boiling water to cover by 1 inch. Bring to a boil, cover, reduce the heat, and simmer for 15 minutes until most of the water has been absorbed. When the vegetables are soft and pulpy, remove and discard the bay leaf and thyme. Reserve the cinnamon.

Using a blender, purée the soup in batches to a creamy consistency. (A food processor will give a less silky texture.) Add the drained rice and milk, then taste and adjust the seasonings. Bring to a boil, simmer for 5 minutes, and serve with thyme sprinkled over the top, and a few reserved shards of the cinnamon, if preferred.

Note: This chowder may be served chilled, with hot garlic or herb bread, or *fougasse*, the lacy Provençal bread.

Buckwheat flour, even in Russia, is usually combined with all-purpose flour for best results. Rice flour is used here instead, giving some tenderness and a mild sweetness to balance the nutty buckwheat taste. This recipe adds the eggs all at once, rather than separating them, and so is quicker and easier.

rice and buckwheat blini

¾ **cup rice flour**

¾ **cup buckwheat flour**

2 teaspoons active dry yeast, or a ½ oz. sachet

2 cups milk

2 tablespoons extra-virgin olive oil

1 tablespoon clear honey

1 teaspoon sea salt flakes

1 egg

6–8 tablespoons olive oil, lard, or clarified butter, for sautéing

Toppings:

a choice of: melted butter and sour cream; crème fraîche (about 2 oz. per person), plus 1 tablespoon scissor-snipped chives; beluga caviar or keta (salmon roe); smoked trout, salmon, halibut, or sturgeon; pickled herring (about 2 oz. per person)

Makes about 48, serves 6 as an appetizer, or 8 as party food

Sift the flours with the dry yeast. Bring the milk to blood heat (a drop on the inside wrist feels barely warm), by heating in a saucepan, or microwaving on HIGH/FULL for about 1½ minutes. Add the oil, honey, and salt, and stir.

Pour this liquid all at once into the dry ingredients. Beat to form a batter the consistency of thick cream. Stand the batter in a warm place for about 20 to 40 minutes (or longer if you have time), until a few bubbles appear. Beat in the egg. Heat one (or two) pancake griddles or heavy-bottom skillets. Add a little oil, lard, or clarified butter. Spoon in 4 pancakes at a time (each about 1 tablespoon). Cook over moderate heat for about 1 minute until bubbles form all around the edges. Flip the pancakes over and cook for a further minute, or until firm and golden. Keep them warm until all are made.

Serve with a selection of the suggested toppings, such as the crème fraîche and chives, and the soured cream and caviar shown here— and a glass of iced vodka.

Note: To speed the cooking process, use two skillets—this way, the blini are done in under 15 minutes and remain velvety and fresh.

This vegetarian version of the classic dish came from a *kafenion* on the Ionian island of Zante where dried fruits are a major crop. Serve these as an appetizer—as part of a mixed *meze* with feta, olives, and pickled chiles, for example—and always with a bowl of authentic, thick Greek plain yogurt. A glass of ouzo is an extra treat.

greek dolmathes

8 oz. fresh vine leaves, or preserved vine leaves, drained (about 50–60)

8 oz. onions, quartered and finely sliced

4 oz. scallions or baby leeks, trimmed and finely sliced

1 large bunch of fresh herbs, such as parsley, mint and/or dill, chopped

⅔ cup extra-virgin olive oil

¾ cup long-grain white rice, soaked briefly in cold water

⅓ cup currants

½ cup pignoli nuts

2 lemons

2½–3 cups boiling vegetable stock

2 teaspoons salt

To Serve:

1 tub Greek yogurt, about 1 cup

2 lemons, cut into wedges

Makes about 45–55, serves 6–8

If using brine-preserved leaves, leave them in a colander under running cold water until the sink is half full. Agitate them, then let drain. If using fresh leaves, blanch 5 to 6 at a time for about 1 minute in a large pan of boiling salted water. Rinse in cold water and drain in a colander.

Mix the onions and scallions or leeks with the herbs, half the oil, and the drained rice. Season to taste. Stir in the currants, nuts, and the juice of 1 lemon. Put 1 heaped teaspoon of filling at the stalk end of each leaf. Roll this end then the two side flaps over towards the center, neatly but not too tightly. Roll up, keeping the seam beneath, leaving room for expansion. Continue until all the filling has been used.

Put half the remaining leaves over the base of a large pan, flameproof casserole, or skillet, overlapping each leaf.

Pack in the dolmathes in concentric circles. Cover with the remaining leaves and a flat, heatproof plate.

Pour in boiling stock until just covered, add the salt, then bring to a boil, cover, reduce the heat, and simmer for about 45 to 55 minutes, or until rice is sticky, swollen, and tender. Let stand undisturbed for 10 minutes. Drain if necessary.

Serve hot or warm, but not chilled. Drizzle with the remaining oil and serve with yogurt and lemon wedges.

paella valenciana
spanish paella
with chicken, shrimp, and squid

Spain's paella is a handsome, one-pan dish. Use a round, short-grain Spanish paella rice such as Bomba, or the famous Calasparra, from Spanish grocers, or an Italian risotto-style rice. Allow two handfuls, or 3 to 4 oz. per person for paella, and cook for about 18 minutes (or 25 to 30 for Calasparra, which may also need more water). The fiercer heat, the lack of stirring and the fact that the rice goes directly into the boiling liquid all make this very different from a risotto.

8 small squid

2 lb. live mussels, scrubbed

⅔ cup white wine

6 tablespoons extra-virgin olive oil

16 uncooked medium shrimp, shell-on, heads removed and reserved for stock (see below)

8 uncooked prawns

1 lb. chicken cut into chunks

1½ lb. chorizo, cut into chunks

1 large Spanish onion, sliced

2 red bell peppers, seeded and sliced

1 whole garlic head, trimmed

2 large fleshy tomatoes, chopped

2 teaspoons sweet paprika

2½ cups paella rice or risotto rice

8 oz. peeled fava beans

1 pinch of saffron threads

6 tablespoons scissor-snipped fresh flat-leaf parsley, to serve (optional)

Fish Stock:

shrimp heads (see above)

2 lb. white fish bones or heads

1 large bouquet garni (sprigs of thyme, bay, flat-leaf parsley, celery, and orange zest, tied together)

2 teaspoons black peppercorns

1 Spanish onion, quartered

2 carrots quartered

1¼ cups medium white wine

6 cups cold water

1–2 teaspoons sea salt

Serves 8

1 To make the stock, put all the ingredients except the salt in a pan, bring to a boil, and simmer for 10 to 15 minutes. Skim several times. Strain back into the rinsed pan. Continue simmering for 15 to 20 minutes. Season to taste.

2 To prepare the squid, gently pull apart the head and body. Cut off and reserve the tentacles. Remove and discard the plastic-like stiffener and soft innards from the body. Remove the skin if preferred.

3 Discard any open mussels. Put in a pan with the white wine. Boil fiercely, covered, until they open (about 1 to 2 minutes). Remove one by one and set aside. Strain the liquid into the fish stock, producing about 6 cups total.

4 Heat half the oil in a large paella pan or skillet. Add the shrimp, prawns, and squid and sauté briefly until barely set. Remove and set aside. Add the chicken and chorizo, and brown over moderate heat for 10 to 12 minutes.

5 Add the onion, bell peppers, garlic, tomatoes, stock and half the paprika. Bring to a rapid boil, stir in the rice, reduce the heat to a gentle simmer and cook, uncovered, without stirring, for 16 to 18 minutes, until the rice is cooked.

6 Add the beans, saffron, remaining paprika, and oil. Stir, add the seafood, then cook for 8 to 10 minutes on a very low heat until the rice is fully cooked and dry. Add extra stock or water as necessary. Serve sprinkled with parsley.

Italian risotto is remarkably straightforward if quality ingredients are used. Fresh butter, good risotto rice such as Carnaroli or Arborio, a glass of white wine, and strong, flavorful stock are all essentials.

risotto alla milanese
saffron risotto

6 tablespoons salted butter

1 medium onion, sliced

3–4 garlic cloves, crushed (optional)

2 cups white Italian risotto rice

½ cup white wine

1 large pinch of saffron threads

¼ teaspoon sea salt flakes

(or, if stock is salty, sugar)

4 cups boiling chicken stock

3 oz. fresh Parmesan cheese (or *grana padano*), finely sliced

freshly ground black pepper

sprigs of flat-leaf parsley, to serve

Variation—Wild Mushroom Risotto:

1 oz. dried porcini mushrooms, broken

½ oz. dried morel mushrooms, broken

4 cups boiling chicken stock

½ cup robust red wine

flat-leaf parsley, to serve

(omit the saffron and salt)

Serves 4

Heat 4 tablespoons of the butter in a medium-sized, heavy-bottom saucepan. Add the onion and garlic, if using, sauté gently for 1 minute, then stir in the rice and the wine. Let it bubble away.

Grind the saffron and salt or sugar in a small bowl, then add a ladle of stock. Pour half this mixture into the rice and reserve the remainder. Continue simmering the rice, adding ladles of boiling stock at intervals, until all the liquid is used and absorbed (about 28 minutes). The risotto should be tender but still very rich, moist, and glossy. Alternatively, add all the stock at once and cook over a low heat for 28 to 32 minutes, stirring gently from time to time.

Add the remaining butter and saffron, then stir in some pepper and half the cheese. To serve, sprinkle with the remaining cheese and garnish with sprigs of parsley.

For the mushroom variation, put the mushrooms in a pan and add the hot stock. Simmer, covered, for 10 to 15 minutes, until dark and flavorful. Strain and reserve the liquid. Rinse the mushroom pieces. Proceed as for saffron risotto but omit the saffron and salt or sugar, and use red wine instead of white. The rinsed mushrooms should be cooked with the rice.

spicy camargue rice
with char-grilled duck breasts

Red rice from the Camargue in the South of France is a rogue strain with a pretty red-brown color. A wholegrain rice, chewy and interesting, it seems destined to become a new and fashionable ingredient. Similar red rice strains also grow in other areas, such as India and the American South.

Rub the duck with the garlic, snipped tarragon, honey, and peppercorns. Marinate in a non-reactive dish for 15 minutes. Put the rice in a medium, heavy-bottom pan, cover with the stock, return to a boil, cover, and simmer for 30 minutes. To make the onion confit, put the sliced and blanched onions in a pan with the jelly and vinegar, and stir until the jelly has dissolved and a glaze forms. Set aside.

Oil and preheat a cast-iron stove-stop grill pan or char-grill. When the rice is almost cooked and stock almost completely absorbed, set the four *magrets*, skin sides down, on the grill. Drizzle with the remaining oil. Cook, pressing down firmly with a spatula, for 8 to 10 minutes altogether. The duck surface should be seared and part-caramelized but the center, when pushed with a finger, should still feel semi-soft: it should remain rosy yet be well warmed through. Put the cooked duck breasts on top of the cooked rice and pour over the remaining marinade. Cover the pan again and cook for a further 10 minutes over low heat. Remove the *magrets* and set them aside. Stir most of the onion confit into the rice (drained, if necessary).

To serve, spoon the rice onto heated dinner plates. Slice the duck breasts and arrange on top of the rice, add generous spoonfuls of very cold crème fraîche, a sprig of tarragon, and a trickle of the onion confit, then serve.

4 *magrets de canard* (**Barbary duck breast portions**), **about 2 lb. total**

4 garlic cloves, crushed

8 sprigs of French tarragon, 4 scissor-snipped, and 4 to serve

2 tablespoons clear, scented honey

2 teaspoons green peppercorns, crushed

2 tablespoons extra-virgin olive oil

8 tablespoons crème fraîche, to serve

Spicy Red Camargue Rice:

2 cups red **Camargue long-grain rice** (**or American red rice**)

3 cups boiling duck, chicken, or pork stock

Onion Confit:

2 red onions, thinly sliced, blanched briefly in boiling water and dried

4 tablespoons redcurrant, gooseberry, or guava jelly

2 tablespoons red wine vinegar

Serves 4

This Byzantine-style rich rice stuffing for my Christmas turkey was taught to me by an Athenian political journalist and epicure. It is also good with other kinds of poultry or feathered game, as well as whole turkeys (add to the roasting pan 35 to 40 minutes before the end of the cooking time).

chestnut rice stuffing
with roasted turkey breast

2½ lb. turkey breast joint
extra-virgin olive oil
4 tablespoons Greek ouzo (or raki)
salt and freshly ground black pepper
Chestnut Rice Stuffing:
⅔ cup dried apricots or figs
½ cup walnut halves
½ cup salted, roasted almonds
I small orange
8 tablespoons extra-virgin olive oil
2 onions, chopped
4 garlic cloves, chopped
1¼ cups white long-grain rice
½ cup seedless raisins
12 oz. prepared, cooked, unsweetened chestnuts
¼ cup pignoli nuts
I teaspoon allspice berries, crushed
2 teaspoons ground cinnamon
2 teaspoons dried oregano
I large bunch of flat-leaf parsley, scissor-snipped
3 cups chicken or turkey stock

Serves 6–8

Rub the turkey with oil, salt, and pepper and put in a roasting pan. Roast, uncovered, in a preheated oven, at 375°F. Allow 20 minutes per pound and 20 minutes extra—about 70 minutes in total.

To make the stuffing, first chop the dried fruit, walnuts, almonds, and the orange, including the peel and pith. Heat the oil in a heavy-bottom pan, and sauté the onions, garlic, and rice for 2 minutes, then add the all the stuffing ingredients. Return to a boil, cover, and simmer for 8 minutes or until the rice is par-cooked and much of the liquid absorbed. (The turkey should have been cooking for about 40 minutes.)

Pour the rice stuffing and its liquid around the turkey. Pour in the ouzo. Cover the pan with a double layer of foil, pinching tightly closed all around the edges, or with a tight-fitting lid. Roast for 30 to 35 minutes more.

Uncover the pan and test the turkey for doneness: the juices should run clear and gold, without a trace of pink, when the fleshiest part of the breast is pierced with a knife. (Catch the juices in a metal spoon to show the color.) Leave the turkey and its stuffing, covered, to stand in a warm place for 5 minutes, to develop maximum succulence. Carve in large, even slices. Serve with a mound of the stuffing, either immediately while hot, or chilled the next day. Crisp romaine lettuce hearts and a yogurt-based dressing make excellent accompaniments.

kohlrouladen

stuffed cabbage leaves
with sauerkraut and a red bell pepper sauce

Traditionally, this hearty, oven-baked dish might be served with tomato sauce and green bell peppers. This version uses canned red bell peppers, roasted and peeled, often labeled "pimiento." Both color and flavor remain bright and clear. You could also use char-grilled, peeled bell peppers and fruity vinegar. Sweet red peppers, hot red chiles, and red paprika are all integral to the cuisines of many of Germany's neighboring countries.

1 lb. prepared sauerkraut

½ cup long-grain white rice

1 white cabbage, about 1½–2 lb.

3 onions, chopped

2 teaspoons caraway seeds

1 large bunch of fresh thyme

1½–2 teaspoons salt

1 lb. minced pork, bacon, or ham

½ stick salted butter, cubed

4 ripe tomatoes, chopped

3 oz. tomato purée

2 tablespoons tomato concentrate

about 13 oz. canned roasted, peeled pimientos, chopped

½ teaspoon cayenne pepper

6–8 rindless slices smoked bacon (optional)

Serves 4–5

1 Drain the sauerkraut, and rinse in cold water if very sharp tasting. Squeeze dry and spread half over the base of a large baking dish. Cook the rice in boiling salted water for 10 minutes or until part-cooked. Drain and set aside.

2 Cut the central core out of the cabbage and peel off 16 perfect leaves. Blanch in a large pan of boiling water until limp, 2 at a time (2 to 3 minutes for outer leaves, less for inner ones). Refresh in cold water, then drain.

3 Mix 2 of the onions with the caraway, thyme, salt, a quarter of the pork, and half the remaining sauerkraut. Whizz in a food processor. Knead this mixture with the cooked rice into the remaining pork. Divide into 16 parts.

4 Snip and discard the hard central rib from each leaf. Shape the 16 portions of mixture and put one at the base of each leaf. Roll up, turn and tuck in the side flaps, and continue to roll up like a cork, with the seams underneath.

5 To make the sauce, heat the butter in a pan and cook the remaining onion until golden. Add the tomatoes, tomato purée and concentrate, pimientos, and cayenne. Cook for 3 to 4 minutes. Put in a blender and purée until smooth.

6 Put some of the sauce into a baking pan, add the rolls, sauerkraut, and bacon, if using, cover with foil and cook in a preheated oven at 350°F for 1 hour. Uncover and cook for 30 minutes. Serve drizzled with sauce.

honey rice ice cream
with orange and saffron

½ cup white short-grain pudding rice

2½ cups fresh orange juice

6 oz. clear honey

1 large pinch of powdered saffron

2½ cups heavy cream

1 tablespoon Cointreau, Grand Marnier,
or triple sec liqueur

2 teaspoons fresh orange zest,
cut in fine shreds with a
cannelle knife or zester

Serves 4–6

Combine the rice, 2 cups of the orange juice and ¼ cup water in a medium saucepan. Bring to a boil, reduce the heat, cover, and simmer on the lowest possible heat for about 20 minutes until the rice is tender and the liquid greatly reduced. Stir well, and let cool over ice for 5 to 10 minutes. Stir in the honey, remaining juice, saffron powder, cream, liqueur, and zest, and stir again.

Prepare the ice-cream making machine and, with the paddles turning, pour in the mixture. Churn for 18 to 20 minutes or until the mixture becomes solid enough to make a rhythmic rattling noise as the blade rotates.

Smooth the ice-cream into a 4-cup domed metal bombe mold, Pyrex bowl, or loaf pan. Cover and refreeze the ice cream for 2 hours or longer.

One hour before serving, put in the refrigerator to soften. Remove the lid. Hold warmed, wet cloths around the mold or dip it briefly into hand-hot water. Invert, then turn out the ice cream. Serve in slices with crisp cookies or wafers.

To still-freeze in a home freezer: set freezer to "fast-freeze" on its lowest setting. Pour the mixture into a non-rigid polypropylene 4-cup container. Snap on the lid. Fast-freeze for 1½ hours or until the mixture forms hard crystals around the edge but is soft at the center. Beat the edges into the center using an electric beater. Reseal.

Alternatively, empty the part-set ice cream into a food processor. Process to a uniform slush. Pour back into the container. Reseal. Refreeze for 1½ hours. Repeat the beating. Refreeze for a final 2 hours or so.

An unusual ice cream which, instead of being made of egg-based custard, fruit, and cream, is made of short or round-grain rice cooked in orange juice until it is so tender it forms a jelly-like custard. One caution, however, is that starch-based ices need slow "conditioning" in the fridge for an hour rather than being eaten straight from the freezer (too brittle) or thawed quickly at room temperature (too soft outside, too firm inside). So condition the ice cream in the refrigerator while earlier courses are served. A delicious, easy, exotic recipe.

The cooking traditions of the Middle East are inextricably bound to their historical links with the great civilizations of **Persia** and **Byzantium**. Dishes such as pilafs and pulaus migrated across the world to become paella in Spain and even jambalaya in the USA.

the middle east

A classic dish, usually made in 3 or 4 separate operations, is slightly simplified here into a one-pan dish. A great party dish that looks impressive, but is easy once the initial stages are complete.

zarda palau

chicken pulau with almonds
orange and pistachios

2 oranges, washed and dried*
¾ cup sugar
2 large pinches saffron threads
or 4 pinches saffron powder
½ stick butter or 2 oz. butter ghee
1 cup blanched almonds
4–6 boneless, skinless breasts
of chicken or guinea fowl,
each cut into 4 pieces
2 onions, sliced into rings
2¼ cups white basmati rice
2 oz. pistachio nuts,
blanched and peeled
salt and freshly ground black pepper
6–8 sprigs of mint, to garnish
Serves 4–6

*If minneolas are in season and available, substitute 4 of these for the 2 oranges. Their juice is good, but their zest is superb!

Using a zester or canelle knife, remove the orange zest in long shreds or, alternatively, use a vegetable peeler, then slice the strips into fine shreds. Blanch by pouring boiling water over, then refresh in cold water and drain.

Put the sugar in a pan with the orange zest and about ¾ cup juice, and boil for 5 to 8 minutes, until thick and syrupy. Add the saffron, stir, and set aside.

Heat the butter or butter ghee in a large flameproof casserole. Briefly brown the almonds, remove with a slotted spoon, and set aside. Add the chicken or guinea fowl, brown for about 2 to 3 minutes on each side, then remove and set aside.

Add the onions and cook over moderate heat until softened and translucent. Return the chicken to the pan, add seasonings and 4 cups boiling water, then stir to dissolve the sediment. Stir in the rice and return to a boil. Cover with a lid, reduce to a simmer, then cook gently for 12 to 15 minutes on top of the stove, or 35 to 45 minutes in a preheated oven at 300°F. Remove the lid: the rice should be fairly plump and tender, and the liquid absorbed.

Sprinkle with the almonds, pistachios, and saffron syrup mixture, reserving the zest. Cover and cook again for a further 5 minutes on top of the stove or 10 to 15 minutes in the oven. Add the reserved zest, looping it up attractively on top. Add the mint garnish and serve hot from the casserole.

Crisp salad leaves, bunches of herbs, hot flatbread, and a large bowl of plain yogurt will all make wonderful accompaniments.

The author and Middle Eastern food expert Tess Mallos described this ancient rice dish as one which perfectly satisfied the calorie and blood-sugar needs of Bahrain's pearl divers who dove to considerable depths in hazardous conditions, and sustained each quest for 10 minutes at a time. The combination of richness, sweetness, and savoriness is remarkable and intriguing. Traditionally this dish would be served with lamb or seafood dishes.

pearl divers' rice
with saffron and honey

1 pinch of saffron threads
or 1 large pinch of powdered saffron

8 green cardamom pods, crushed

2 tablespoons rosewater

4 cups boiling lamb or chicken stock

2¼ cups white basmati rice

2 onions, sliced into rings

2 teaspoons salt

3 oz. clear honey

½ stick butter or butter ghee,
chopped into 8 pieces

1 large bunch of fresh parsley, dill, or
mint, scissor-snipped (optional)

Serves 4–6

Combine the saffron, the black seeds from the cardamom pods, rosewater, and 4 tablespoons of the boiling stock in a small heatproof bowl, and set over boiling water while you cook the rice.

Put the rice, onions, and salt in a large, heavy-bottom pan, and pour over the remaining boiling stock. Return to a boil, cover, reduce to a gentle simmer, and cook for 10 minutes or until almost all the liquid has been absorbed.

Pour the saffron-cardamom-rosewater-stock mixture on top and drizzle the honey over the surface. Push 8 holes in the rice down to the base of the pan and add a bit of ghee or butter to each. Cover the pan again and simmer for a further 5 minutes. Remove from the heat, wrap the pan in a cloth, let stand for another 10 minutes, then serve hot, sprinkled with parsley, dill, or mint, if using.

This is an easy, modern update of a traditional long-cooked Iranian dish. The spice seasoning, *baharat*, is an important component: use the extra with other dishes. Keep it airtight in a screwtop jar or lidded china pot and bring it to the table as a condiment for sprinkling.

lamb and rice sausage
with parsley, lime, and spices

I large bunch of flat-leaf parsley
I large bunch of fresh cilantro
I lb. twice-minced lamb
4 garlic cloves, crushed
I onion, finely sliced
2 teaspoons sea salt
2 tablespoons ground cinnamon
8 oz. cooked brown rice
2½ cups boiling lamb stock
I large bunch of parsley stems, crushed
zest (in big pieces) and juice
of I lime
Baharat Seasoning:
I tablespoon black peppercorns
I tablespoon coriander seeds
I tablespoon cumin seeds
I tablespoon cloves
I cinnamon stick
2 tablespoons hot paprika
½ nutmeg, freshly ground
Serves 4

Scissor-snip the parsley and cilantro. Mix with the lamb, garlic, onion, salt, cinnamon, and cooked rice. Knead to make a dense, smooth paste then divide into 6 pieces. Using clean hands, roll out each piece to about 8 inches long. Coil this up on a flat, heatproof plate, such as Pyrex. Continue shaping the lengths of sausage, joining each new section firmly to the last using a fork. The completed coil should be about 12 inches in diameter. Put a deep, heavy-bottom skillet or shallow flameproof casserole upside down over the plate, then invert both—the sausage will be compressed by the plate as it cooks.

Pour the boiling stock over the sausage in the skillet, crush the parsley stems, and add to the pan together with the lime zest. Bring the pan back to a boil (8 to 10 minutes), reduce to a steady simmer, cover, and cook for 20 minutes more.

To make the *baharat* seasoning, put all the ingredients in an electric spice grinder or food processor, and whizz. Reserve 2 tablespoons for this dish and store the rest for later use in other dishes.

When the sausage is cooked, strain off the liquid. Put a plate over the pan, invert both, then remove the pan. Slide the sausage off the plate and on to a serving dish. Pour over the lime juice and sprinkle with the *baharat*. Serve with crisp green leafy salad and buttered or saffron-scented rice.

Note: Brown rice cooks particularly quickly in a pressure cooker. Allow about 15 to 20 minutes, (about a third of the usual cooking time), following the manufacturer's instructions.

stuffed vegetables
with rice and sour cherries

Persian seasonings are fascinating and refreshing. This dish has a spicing mixture which hinges on pepper, cinnamon, and mint (known as *nano dok*), together with turmeric, cumin, and sumak, a red-brown souring powder. Dried barberries or dried sour cherries can be difficult to find, so dried cranberries could be used instead. However, all these ingredients are available in Middle Eastern foodstores, Iranian grocers, specialist delis, and the more enlightened supermarkets! Both short and long-grain white rice (basmati is a favorite) work well in this simple but delicious vegetable dish.

4 large beefsteak tomatoes, with the tops sliced off and reserved
4 large red bell peppers with stems
2 tablespoons butter ghee or clarified butter
2 garlic cloves, chopped
2 onions, chopped
8 oz. twice-minced lamb
2 cinnamon sticks, crushed
1 teaspoon ground turmeric
1 teaspoon cumin seeds, crushed
1 teaspoon cracked black pepper
1 teaspoon sumak (optional)
2 oz. dried sour cherries, barberries, or cranberries
½ cup white short-grain, basmati, or other long-grain rice
½ cup bulgar (burghul, or cracked wheat)
3 cups lamb or chicken stock
½ teaspoon salt
2 teaspoons dried mint or 2 tablespoons sliced fresh mint
To Serve (optional):
8 sprigs of mint
8 oz. sheep or goat's milk yogurt
lavash, taftoon, pita, or other Middle Eastern flatbreads
Serves 4

1 Scoop the tomato pulp and seeds into a blender. Halve the bell peppers and remove and discard the seeds and membranes. Roast the vegetable halves in a preheated oven at 400°F for 10 minutes.

2 Meanwhile heat the ghee or butter in a heavy-bottom skillet and sauté the garlic, onions, minced lamb, cinnamon sticks, turmeric, cumin, pepper, and sumak, if using, for 5 to 6 minutes over high heat, stirring regularly.

3 Whizz the tomato pulp and seeds in the blender, and add to the pan together with the dried fruit, rice, bulgar wheat, and 2½ cups of the stock. Season with salt. Return to a boil, cover, then simmer for 10 minutes.

4 Spoon the mixture into the vegetable shells and spoon 1 tablespoon of reserved stock over each. Set the sliced tops back on top of the tomatoes. Cover the dish with double layer of foil and return to the oven.

5 Reduce the oven heat to 350°F and cook for about 40 to 45 minutes or until the rice is plumped up, all liquid is absorbed, and the vegetables are sweetly aromatic.

6 Serve hot with a spoonful of yogurt on top if desired (remove the tops of the tomatoes first then replace at an angle). Sprinkle with fresh or dried mint and serve with sprigs of mint and flatbreads to mop up the juices.

Traditionally this dish used almond "milk" obtained from grinding blanched almonds, infusing them in liquid, then squeezing out their liquid to use in the dish. The almonds were then discarded. Almonds are expensive, so I infuse them, but do not discard them. This gives a slightly grittier, grainier version, but delicious nonetheless. Some people loathe the marzipan taste of almond essence, so you could use Noyau or Amaretto liqueur instead.

keskül
almond rice custard
with berries or pomegranate seeds

3 cups milk
1 cup very fresh ground almonds
1 large pinch of salt
⅓ cup ground rice
⅔ cup light cream
6 tablespoons sugar
⅛–¼ teaspoon almond essence or
2–3 teaspoons Noyau liqueur
To Serve:
1 ripe pomegranate, or
6 oz. soft berries, such as
blackberries, mulberries,
red or white currants
1 oz. pistachio nuts or toasted almond
flakes (optional)
2 tablespoons confectioners sugar
(optional)
Serves 4–6

Boil 1 cup of the milk until frothing, pour onto the ground almonds, stir well, then pour the mixture into a blender or food processor. Whizz for 10 seconds.

Mix the salt, ground rice, and cream. Heat the remaining milk until frothing. Pour onto the ground rice and cream mixture, then beat. Return to the pan, bring to a boil, then simmer, stirring, for 2 to 3 minutes or until thickened. Add the unstrained almond-milk mixture, and the sugar.

Continue cooking and stirring briefly, then remove from the heat. Cool the custard over iced water. When almost cold stir in the almond essence or liqueur to suit your taste. Pour into 4 to 6 small dishes, bowls or glasses. Chill.

If using a pomegranate, break it open, remove the clumps of red seeds, and sprinkle a pile in the center of each bowl. If using berries, remove the stems, and place in the same way. Sprinkle with nuts and dust with confectioners sugar, if using. Serve warm, cool, or chilled: it thickens more on standing. Crisp cookies would also be suitable accompaniments.

From Morocco to the Cape, from **West Africa to Zanzibar**, African cuisines are enormously diverse. They range from the **Islamic-influenced** dishes of North Africa, to the Indian-spiced curries of the east coasts, and the **traditions** brought to the Americas on slave ships.

africa

Spice-trading nations like Portugal, India, and Iraq have had strong influences on the varied and lively cuisine of the eastern coast of Africa. This simple curry uses good-quality curry paste and a purée of sun-dried tomatoes, which produces interesting effects. Use white fish such as gurnard, snapper, or bream. Use a nonstick pan so the rice will reheat perfectly without sticking.

tanzanian fish curry
with mustard seed rice

4 pieces white fish, about 6 oz. each

1 tablespoon turmeric

1 teaspoon sea salt flakes

3 tablespoons peanut oil

2 onions, sliced into rings

2 garlic cloves, crushed

2 tablespoons medium-hot curry paste

3 tablespoons sun-dried tomato paste

2 green jalapeño or serrano chiles

2 limes

about 1¾ cups canned coconut milk

Mustard Seed Rice:

2 tablespoons peanut oil

4 garlic cloves, crushed

1–2 tablespoons black mustard seeds

1 cinnamon stick, crushed (optional)

1½ lb. cooked white long-grain rice

3–4 tablespoons seasoned fish stock

Serves 4

Pat the fish dry with paper towels, then rub in the turmeric and salt. Heat the oil in a large pan and brown the fish briefly on both sides. Remove the fish from the pan. Add the onions and garlic, sauté until browned, then sauté the curry paste and tomato paste for 1 to 2 minutes. Halve the chiles lengthwise and seed, then add them to the pan together with the juice of 1 of the limes. Cook another 2 minutes, taking care not to burn. Add the coconut milk and heat to simmering. Add the fish and poach for 5 to 6 minutes on each side, adding a little water if the sauce becomes too thick.

To prepare the rice, heat the oil in a nonstick pan and sauté the garlic, seeds, and cinnamon, if using, until the seeds start to pop and the garlic and cinnamon are aromatic. Add the rice and stir-fry, moving it constantly, for 3 to 4 minutes. Add the well-seasoned stock, cover the pan, and heat the rice through.

Serve the seeded rice in deep bowls, with the curry spooned over. Garnish with the remaining lime, cut into wedges or chunks.

Flavorful chicken, stewed in a tomato, peanut, and chile sauce, is a West African favorite. This Mali version has brilliant orange-red dendé oil (palm oil) stirred into both the stew and the rice. Vivid color and a strange, pungent earthy flavor is the result. If no palm oil is available (try ethnic markets and Afro-Caribbean grocers) substitute a little extra peanut oil mixed with annatto powder or even turmeric.

chicken and peanut stew
with red dendé rice

2½ lb. chicken

1 teaspoon cayenne pepper

1–2 teaspoons salt

1 tablespoon ground ginger

1 tablespoon mild paprika

2 tablespoons peanut oil

2 onions, each cut into 8 wedges

4 garlic cloves, chopped

13 oz. canned tomatoes in juice

4 ripe tomatoes, cut into chunks

1 large bunch of fresh oregano,
or 1½ teaspoons dried

4 tablespoons crunchy peanut butter

4 cups hot chicken stock

2 cups white long-grain rice

2–3 tablespoons red dendé (palm) oil

1 lemon or lime, cut in 4 wedges

Serves 4–6

Cut the chicken into 10 to 12 pieces. Combine the cayenne, salt, ginger, and paprika in a bowl, add the chicken, and turn until well coated. Heat the peanut oil in a large deep flameproof pan, add half the chicken, and sauté for about 3 to 4 minutes or until browned. Remove the browned chicken pieces from the pan and keep them warm. Repeat with the remaining chicken, remove, and keep it warm. Sauté the onion and garlic briefly, then return all the chicken to the pan. Chop the canned tomatoes, and add them to the pan together with the fresh tomatoes, oregano (keeping a few sprigs for garnish, if fresh), peanut butter, and 1¼ cups of the hot chicken stock. Return to a boil, reduce to a simmer, part-cover the pan, and cook for 30 minutes.

Meanwhile put the rice in a medium, heavy-bottom saucepan together with the remaining hot stock. Return to a boil, cover, reduce the heat to very low, and cook for another 12 minutes or until all liquid is absorbed. Stir in about 1 to 2 tablespoons of the dendé oil and set aside.

Add the remaining dendé oil to the stew, and stir well. Serve the stew and rice together with a wedge of lemon or lime and a sprig of oregano, if using.

couscous

moroccan couscous
with rice, lemon, and tahini

A simplified version of the classic Moroccan dish *Couscous aux Sept Légumes*—use zucchinis, pattypan squash, or both. Pickled lemons, instant couscous, and harissa, the fiery red North African spice paste can be found in North African, Middle Eastern, and French grocers, ethnic foodstores, and good supermarkets.

Halve the zucchinis lengthwise and the squash crosswise. Peel and seed the cucumber and cut into chunks. Slice the carrots diagonally. Mix the chermoula ingredients in a bowl, add the vegetables and toss until well coated. Let stand. Put the rice and hot stock into a medium, heavy-bottom pan, return to a boil, cover, reduce to a simmer, and cook, undisturbed, for 6 minutes. Stir in the couscous and arrange the vegetables evenly on top. Sprinkle over the remaining chermoula and other juices.

Cover and cook, undisturbed, for a further 8 to 10 minutes or until the vegetables are succulent and tender, the couscous and rice are cooked, and all the liquid is absorbed. Reserve 3 to 4 sprigs of the mint and chop the rest. Put the vegetables on one side of the serving dish. Stir the olives, lemon pieces (or zest), and chopped mint through the rice-couscous mix. Spoon onto the serving dish beside the vegetables, and let cool slightly. To make the tahini sauce, put the garlic, cumin, tahini, and lemon juice in a blender, and purée to a thick cream. Trickle in 8 to 10 tablespoons iced water, a spoonful at a time to form a pale creamy dressing. To serve, trickle the sauce over the salad (warm or cool, but not chilled), add the reserved mint sprigs, and serve the remaining dressing separately. Delicious!

8–12 baby zucchinis or pattypan squash
½ cucumber
4 carrots
1¼ cups white long-grain rice
3¾ cups hot, seasoned vegetable stock
4 oz. "instant" couscous
Chermoula Marinade:
2 garlic cloves, chopped
2 teaspoons harissa paste
1 teaspoon powdered cumin
1 teaspoon mild paprika
1 bunch of fresh cilantro, snipped
6 tablespoons fruity olive oil
Tahini Sauce:
2 garlic cloves, crushed
1 teaspoon cumin
4 oz. tahini (roasted sesame) paste
juice of 2 lemons
To Serve:
3½ oz. small black olives
½ preserved lemon, diced, or lemon zest
1 large bunch of fresh mint
Serves 4

It was in India, many centuries ago, that rice was first parboiled to increase its hardness and keeping qualities, as well as its nutritional value—a crucial consideration in a country where **vegetarianism** is very much part of the **cultural** and **religious** tradition.

india, pakistan, and sri lanka

orange and pumpkin pulao
with two cashumbers and a raita

Rice is the staple food of much of India. The best-known varieties are the short, fine-grained *jeera*, the parboiled *golden sela* basmati, good for pulaos, the fruity scented *ambre mohue* from Maharashtra, and *punni*, a long-grain rice from Tamil Nadu. Basmati rice, originally from Afghanistan, now grows in the Punjab, Haryana, the foothills of the Himalayas, and Uttar Pradesh, as well as in Pakistan, the US, and Thailand, though there are slight regional differences. It is used for ceremonial dishes because it is more expensive. Year-old basmati is much prized—some gourmets age their rice as connoisseurs age wines.

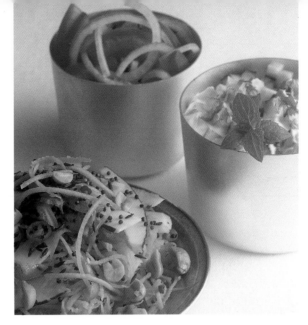

2 oz. butter ghee

1 onion, sliced

1 cup basmati rice

1 fresh bay leaf, bruised

1 cinnamon stick

4 cloves

12 cardamom pods, crushed

8 oz. peeled, seeded pumpkin

finely sliced zest and juice of 2 oranges

Carrot and Coconut Cashumber:

3 oz. fresh coconut

or 3 tablespoons dried coconut

8 oz. carrots, coarsely grated

½ cup roasted peanuts, chopped

juice of 2 limes

½ teaspoon salt

2 chiles, seeded and chopped

2 tablespoons peanut oil

1 teaspoon cumin seeds

1 teaspoon black mustard seeds

Onion and Tomato Cashumber:

2 red onions, finely sliced

2 tomatoes, sliced

1 teaspoon toasted sesame seeds

1 tablespoon soft brown sugar

Cucumber Raita:

½ cucumber, diced

2 cloves garlic, crushed

1 tablespoon chopped fresh mint

½ cup thick plain yogurt

1 tablespoon peanut oil

1 tablespoon mustard seeds

Serves 4

Heat the butter ghee in a pan, add the onion, and sauté to a deep golden brown. Add the rice, bay leaf, cinnamon, cloves, and the black seeds from the cardamom pods, and sauté for another 2 minutes.

Cut the pumpkin into ½-inch dice, and add to the pan with 2 cups of boiling salted water. Return to a boil, cover, and reduce the heat to as low as possible. Cook, undisturbed, for about 10 minutes. Add the orange zest and juice, cover, cook for 2 to 3 minutes more, turn off the heat, and let stand.

To make the carrot and coconut cashumber, grate the fresh coconut. If no fresh coconut is available, use dried coconut, briefly blanched in boiling water, then drained. Mix in a bowl with the carrots, chopped peanuts, lime juice, salt, and chiles, and stir well.

In a separate pan heat 2 tablespoons of peanut oil (or mustard oil if you can find it). Add the cumin seeds and black mustard seeds, heat until they start to pop, then pour over the cashumber.

To make the onion and tomato cashumber, put the sliced onion in a heatproof bowl, and pour boiling water over. Refresh under cold water and pat dry on paper towels. Mix in a small serving bowl together with the sliced tomato, sesame seeds, and brown sugar.

To make the raita, mix the cucumber in a bowl with the garlic, mint, and yogurt. Heat the peanut (or mustard) oil in a small pan, add the mustard seeds, and sauté briefly until they pop. Spoon over the raita.

Serve the two cashumbers and the raita as accompaniments to the pulao.

Many of the pilafs and biryanis from Gujerat, in north-west India, contain ambitious spice combinations, a legacy of its place on an ancient caravan route with famed culinary wealth and riches. It is largely vegetarian, and rice dishes are often made with nuts and dried fruits. Asafoetida, a common Indian spice, stinks on its own, but has the uncanny ability to enhance other flavors.

spicy seeded pilaf
with okra and spinach

1 onion

8 oz. pattypan squash

1–1½ teaspoons hot chile powder

½ teaspoon ground turmeric

2 tablespoons peanut oil or ghee

1 teaspoon poppy seeds, crushed

1 teaspoon cumin seeds, crushed

1 teaspoon coriander seeds, crushed

½ teaspoon asafoetida (optional)

4 garlic cloves, crushed

¼ teaspoon salt

1¼ cups white basmati rice

2½ cups boiling vegetable stock

2 dried bay leaves (optional)

1 oz. creamed coconut, chopped, or ½ cup coconut cream

4 oz. okra, trimmed

4 oz. baby spinach

4 oz. fresh green peas (optional)

2 oz. coconut shreds (fresh or dried)

Serves 4

Slice the onion lengthwise into thin segments. Toss the onion and pattypans in the chile and turmeric. Heat the oil and sauté the vegetables for 1 to 2 minutes or until aromatic. Add the poppy, cumin, and coriander seeds, the asafoetida, garlic, and salt. Cook over moderate heat until the seeds begin to crackle and pop and become aromatic.

Stir in the rice. Sauté for another minute, stirring gently, then add the stock, bay leaves, if using, and the creamed coconut or coconut cream. Cover and reduce the heat to simmering, then cook undisturbed for 8 minutes.

Add the okra, spinach, green peas, and coconut shreds. Cover and cook for a further 4 to 5 minutes until the rice is tender but dry. Remove the bay leaves, stir well and serve the rice with meat, poultry, or fish curries, and accompaniments such as the cashumbers and raita on page 83.

Mild and creamy Indian kormas are a legacy of Moghul rule in India. Their elegance and opulence demonstrate their grand, imperial past—and make them perfect special-occasion dishes.

chicken korma
with pistachio basmati rice

8 oz. sweet potato, sliced

8 oz. baby corn cobs

4 oz. sugar snap peas

4 oz. French beans

1 teaspoon white peppercorns

2 teaspoons sea salt flakes

20 green cardamom pods

2 tablespoons white poppy seeds

4 garlic cloves, finely sliced

1 oz. fresh ginger, finely sliced

½ teaspoon ground turmeric

¼–½ teaspoon cayenne pepper

1 cup cashews

1 cup pignoli nuts

1¾ cups coconut milk

3½ oz. thick, plain Greek yogurt

2 tablespoons lime pickle

1 spicy stock cube, crumbled

12 oz. cooked, boneless chicken, cut into ½-inch cubes

Pistachio Basmati Rice:

2¼ cups basmati rice

¼ cup pistachio nuts

6 tablespoons torn cilantro leaves

Serves 4–6

Put the sweet potato and baby corn in a pan of boiling water and parboil for 3 minutes. Drain. Blanch the sugar snap peas and French beans for 1 minute, cool under running water, then drain. Using a mortar and pestle, pound the peppercorns, salt and cardamom pods. Discard the empty green pods, and reserve the black seeds. Put the mortar contents in a food processor with the white poppy seeds, garlic, ginger, turmeric, cayenne pepper, half the cashews, and half the pignoli nuts. Whizz to a rough paste. Add the coconut milk, thick Greek yogurt, and lime pickle. Whizz again until fairly smooth.

Pour into a large pan, bring to a boil, reduce the heat, and simmer for 5 minutes, adding the crumbled stock cube, 1¼ cups of boiling water, and remaining cashews (but not the pignoli nuts).

Add the parboiled corn cobs and sweet potato to the sauce, together with the blanched peas and beans, and the chicken cubes. Simmer for 3 to 4 minutes, until fragrant and hot.

Bring the rice to a boil in double its volume of boiling salted water. Simmer, covered, for 12 minutes, or until all the water is absorbed. Blanch, peel, and sliver the pistachios, then add to the rice together with the cilantro and remaining pignoli nuts. Leave the rice to stand for 1 to 2 minutes. Serve with the korma.

gosht biryani
lamb biryani
with cilantro and cinnamon

Another elegant culinary result of Moghul rule in India. Because the lamb must first be cooked until tender (and the stock used to cook the rice), this stage can be done well in advance, even the day before. Indian cooks always cut their onions into wedges lengthwise, a method that produces pretty shapes and good caramelized edges, and is also worth using in Western-style dishes. Serve this dish with accompaniments such a spicy sambal or mango chutney.

2 whole green chiles, pierced
2 lb. boneless leg of lamb
3 cups water or stock
1 bunch of cilantro stems
2 inches fresh ginger, sliced
2 cinnamon sticks, crushed
1 teaspoon salt, or to taste
1 stick clarified butter or ghee
4 onions, sliced into wedges
black seeds from 2 teaspoons crushed green cardamom pods
1 teaspoon cloves
½ teaspoon ground turmeric
2 teaspoons cumin seeds, crushed
2 teaspoons coriander seeds
2 red or yellow bell peppers, quartered, seeded, and cored
3 oz. cauliflower florets
6 oz. zucchinis
1½ cups white basmati rice
4 garlic cloves, finely sliced
1 large pinch of saffron threads
1 cup pistachio nuts
1 large bunch of cilantro
Serves 4

1 Place the first 5 ingredients and 1 cinnamon stick in a large saucepan. Bring to a boil, cover, and reduce a simmer. Cook for 1¼ to 1½ hours until the lamb is very tender. Remove and cube the lamb. Measure 2½ cups of stock.

2 Heat the butter or ghee in a pan and sauté the onion 2 to 3 minutes until golden. Add the remaining spices and sauté over a moderate heat until the seeds begin to pop. Remove the onions with a slotted spoon and set aside.

3 Add the bell pepper, cauliflower, and zucchini pieces to the pan, and sauté for 1 to 2 minutes. Remove with a slotted spoon. Add the rice and garlic. Stir over moderate heat for 2 minutes, until coated with butter and spices.

4 Transfer the rice mixture to a large saucepan, then add layers of the onion, lamb and spiced vegetables. Pour in the lamb stock, return a boil, then reduce to a gentle simmer.

5 Sprinkle in the saffron threads, cover with a lid, and cook for 15 minutes or until all the liquid is absorbed. Shell the pistachio nuts and add to the pan with the cilantro. Cover with a lid, and turn off the heat.

6 Cover the pan with a cloth, then let stand, covered, for 10 minutes on top of the stove. Alternatively, put the pan in a preheated oven at 350°F for 10 minutes. Serve with chutneys and a raita.

A recipe with ingredients typical of the former Portuguese colony of Goa; olive oil, cashews, and pork. Pork is forbidden to Muslims and cattle are sacred to Hindus, but both are acceptable to the many Goans who are Christians, and their fine cuisine includes both pork and beef. Most Indian cooks would make their own garam masala, but it is also widely available in Asian stores.

gingered pork chop masala
with cashew rice

2 inches fresh ginger
1 small medium-hot red chile
1 onion, chopped
4 garlic cloves, crushed
1 teaspoon garam masala
6 tablespoons fresh lemon juice
1 teaspoon turmeric powder
1 teaspoon salt
2 tablespoons brown sugar
1 large bunch of fresh mint
4–6 boneless pork chops, about 1½ lb.
2 tablespoons virgin olive oil
⅔ cup fresh orange juice
4 tablespoons thick coconut milk
8 tablespoons thick yogurt
Cashew Rice:
1 cup patna or basmati rice
2 cups boiling meat or chicken stock
1 cup roasted, salted cashews
Serves 4

Peel the ginger and slice finely. Seed the chile and chop finely. Put the ginger, chile, onion, garlic, garam masala, lemon juice, turmeric, salt, sugar, and half the mint in a blender or food processor and blend to a thick purée. Reserve half and pour the remainder over the pork. Let marinate while you cook the rice.

Put the rice in a pan with the boiling stock, bring to a boil, reduce to a simmer, cover the pan, and cook, undisturbed, for 12 to 15 minutes or until tender. (The liquid should be completely absorbed, and the rice tender.)

Heat the oil in a skillet and cook the marinated pork for 3 to 4 minutes on each side. Add the orange juice, cover, and cook gently for 3 to 4 minutes longer. Stir in the coconut milk and 2 tablespoons yogurt and simmer until creamy.

Put the cashews and 2 tablespoons of the remaining yogurt in the food processor with most of the remaining mint (leave the best sprigs for garnish). Blend to a creamy purée, then stir into the rice, together with the reserved marinade. Serve the pork and its sauce over the cashew-rice, sprinkle with the reserved sprigs of mint, and trail the remaining yogurt over the top.

Serve with chapattis, green beans or okra, a dhaal of split peas, perhaps, and a cool, crisp green salad.

Note: Palm sugar or jaggery may be substituted for the brown sugar, and lime juice for the lemon juice, if preferred.

Best-known of India's superb condensed milk puddings is *kheer*, though regional versions have other names. Holy texts tell of these dishes being offered to the gods. Cardamom, pistachio nuts, rose or almond essence, and Indian kewra water (made from pandanus leaves) may also be added, as well as sugar in various forms. A sumptuous dessert, wonderful served warm, cool, or chilled. Varak—real silver, hand-beaten into paper-fine sheets—is available from Asian delis or specialist grocers. It adds drama to this already exotic dish.

kheer rice pudding
with cardamom and pignoli nuts

3 tablespoons butter ghee
or sweet butter
1½ oz. white basmati rice,
washed, drained, and air-dried
2 fresh bay leaves, crushed
8 cups whole milk
½ cup light brown sugar
½ cup currants or raisins
12 green cardamom pods, crushed,
pods discarded, black seeds reserved
¼ cup toasted pignoli nuts
1–2 sheets thin silver foil (varak)
(optional, for special occasions)

Serves 4

Heat the butter ghee or butter over moderate heat in a large, wide, heavy-bottom, preferably nonstick 5-quart saucepan. Stir-fry the rice until it darkens to pale gold, then add the bay leaves and milk. Increase the heat to high and, stirring constantly, bring to a frothing boil (about 10 to 12 minutes). Reduce the heat slightly to medium high.

Let the milk boil for another 35 to 40 minutes, until reduced to about half the original volume. Add sugar, currants, and cardamom, and continue to cook on a low heat, stirring often, for another 15 to 20 minutes, until reduced to about ⅓ to ¼ of its original volume. Stir and cool over iced water, then chill. Decorate with nuts and silver foil, if using, lifting the foil on its attached tissue paper, inverting it over the pudding, then pulling off the amount needed using a fine brush. The pieces do not need to be immaculate—fragments look good.

Rice flour is used here with an equal quantity of all-purpose flour, giving a delicate crispness to these little biscuits. They are delicious with coffee or mint tea, or served with ice creams, custards, or sorbets. Edible ricepaper is often used in cooking or wrapping cookies or sweets.

elaiche gaja

spiced shortbread cookies
with rosewater and pistachios

2 sticks salted butter, at room temperature

1 teaspoon black cardamom seeds (from 8–10 green cardamom pods, lightly crushed)

½ cup sugar

1¼ cups rice flour

1¼ cups all-purpose flour

¼ cup blanched, peeled pistachios, finely slivered or chopped

¼ teaspoon salt

¼ teaspoon baking powder

1 teaspoon double strength rosewater or almond essence

2–3 sheets ricepaper (optional)

2 teaspoons blanched pistachios, slivered, to decorate

Makes 32

Cut the butter into small pieces, and put in a food processor with the black cardamom seeds. Work them together in small bursts, gradually adding the sugar through the feed tube until the mixture becomes light and fluffy.

Mix the rice and plain flours with the chopped pistachios, salt, and baking powder. Add a quarter of this mixture at a time down the feed tube, using the pulse button, until a soft crumbly dough results. Alternatively, use a bowl and a beater. Turn out the dough onto a floured work surface and mix in the rosewater by hand. Put the dough on a sheet of teflon fabric, or ricepaper, and pat out into a rectangle about 8 x 10 inches. Using a knife, cut halfway through the dough into 32 evenly sized rectangles, about 1 x 2 inches each. Prick all over with a fork. Sprinkle a few slivers of pistachio over each biscuit, then bake in a preheated oven at 250°F for 1 hour, or until pale gold, crisp, but not deep brown.

Remove from the oven and separate each biscuit, cutting cleanly through the ricepaper as well, if used. Cool on a wire rack and, when completely cold, store in an airtight container.

spicy coconut loaf
with cashews and cardamom

A densely textured cake, based on a Sri Lankan recipe. You can vary the spices, chopped almonds or walnuts could replace the cashews, and lemon zest and juice can be used instead of orange. This cake can also double as a quick dessert, served with snowy coconut sorbet.

Grease and paper-line a 1 lb. loaf pan (about 5 x 8 x 3 inches). Put the coconut and water in a blender (in 2 batches, if necessary) and whizz until creamy. Set aside.

Using an electric mixer, beat the egg yolks, 1 tablespoon of the coconut mixture, and the sugar until light and fluffy. Add the remaining coconut mixture, and beat well by hand. Sift in the flour, ground rice, and baking powder, then add the black cardamom seeds, spices, orange flower water, cashews, and orange zest—but not the juice—and stir well. Beat the egg whites in a clean bowl until they form stiff peaks. Add the second measure of sugar and beat again until the meringue is stiff and shiny. Fold it gently into the coconut mixture. Pour into the prepared loaf pan. Put towards the top of a preheated oven and bake at 325°F for 1 hour 10 minutes, or until risen and golden brown on top. A skewer inserted in the center of the loaf should come out clean.

Pour the juice over the top. Let stand 15 minutes, then turn out of the pan onto a wire rack. Cool a little. Serve warm, or store in an airtight container.

butter, for greasing
1½ cups shredded coconut
1½ cups water
2 eggs, separated
1 cup plus 1 tablespoon sugar
¾ cup self-rising flour
1 cup plus 2 tablespoons ground rice
1 teaspoon baking powder
12 green cardamom pods, crushed, black seeds reserved, pods discarded
½ teaspoon ground cloves
½ teaspoon ground cinnamon
½ teaspoon ground nutmeg
1 teaspoon double-strength orange flower water
¾ cup cashews, chopped
finely sliced zest and juice of 1 orange (keep separate)
2 tablespoons superfine sugar
Makes 1 lb. loaf

the far east
and southeast asia

Rice is a staple food in China, Japan, and Southeast Asia, and has achieved an almost **mythic status**. Few meals would be complete without rice in one of its many forms—as the original grain, or as noodles, wrappers, vinegar, or even wine. Rice cooking in these regions has achieved the status of **high art**.

classic cantonese fried rice
with scallions, ham, and crab

This casual home-style dish is easy to make as long as the rice has been recently cooked and is cool (neither chilled nor still hot) and you keep the eggs creamy. My version uses ham and crab, chile and black bean sauces, as well as tomato juice to give a rosy effect. Stirring sauces through the rice, rather than serving them separately, is regarded as sacrilege by purists, but it is commonplace, even so. Try other protein foods in place of the crab and ham, as in the variations listed. Use the dish as a basis of experimentation— this is a good-natured dish!

4 oz. cooked, shelled crabmeat

4 oz. cooked smoked ham

4 oz. canned water chestnuts

8 scallions

4 tablespoons peanut,
corn, or safflower oil

2 onions, chopped

1½ lb. cooked, cool, long-grain white
rice (from 2½ cups raw rice)

3 eggs, beaten

2 tablespoons black bean sauce

2 tablespoons fish sauce,
such as nam pla or nuoc mam

1 tablespoon sweet chile sauce,
or garlic-chile sauce

1 tablespoon passata or tomato juice

1 large bunch of flat-leaf parsley

salt and freshly ground pepper

Variations:

Smoked Fish Fried Rice:

4 oz. smoked sturgeon or halibut

4 oz. prosciutto

1 large bunch of chives

Chicken, Smoked Seafood, and
Tarragon Fried Rice:

4 oz. cooked chicken

4 oz. smoked oysters, mussels, or eel

1 large bunch of tarragon

Serves 4–5

Finely slice the crabmeat and smoked ham, drain and slice the water chestnuts, and finely slice the scallions diagonally. Set them aside until you are ready to assemble the dish.

Heat a wok or deep-sided skillet. Add the oil and, when hot, add the onions and sauté over a medium heat until translucent. Add the crabmeat and ham and cook for a further 2 minutes, uncovered, until hot.

Add the cooked rice, heat and stir, then cover and cook, undisturbed, for about 5 minutes, or until heated through. Add the water chestnuts.

Season the eggs with salt and pepper and pour them into a hollow in the center of the rice. Stir around the edges, until just beginning to set, then stir the egg from the middle to the outer edge so the egg sets quickly, but is still moist.

Add the three sauces and passata or tomato juice to the rice, then add the scallions, tossing quickly into the hot rice.

To serve, scissor-snip the parsley, then sprinkle it over the dish. Serve hot while the egg is still creamy: the mixture will continue cooking on the plate.

Variations:

To make the Smoked Fish Fried Rice, cut the smoked sturgeon or halibut into pieces, and substitute for the crab. Slice the prosciutto and substitute for the ham. Snip the chives and use instead of the parsley. Proceed as in the main recipe, keeping the sauces the same.

The Chicken, Smoked Seafood, and Tarragon Fried Rice is an excellent use for leftover roast chicken. Shred the chicken finely, then proceed as in the main recipe, substituting chicken instead of the ham. Use smoked oysters, mussels, or eel instead of the crab, and scissor-snipped tarragon instead of the parsley. Use the same sauces as in the main recipe.

Note: White, long-grain rice is traditionally used to make fried rice, and purists insist it should stay snowy white. However, I have also cooked it with brown rice, which tastes very good indeed.

Crispy fritters with interesting ingredients found at Caribbean markets, Asian grocers, and larger supermarkets. Serve with two dipping sauces: a Sweet-sour dip containing 4 tablespoons rice vinegar, a little chopped scallion, and garlic, plus salt, pepper, and sugar to taste. Make a Chile-sesame dip with 4 tablespoons rice vinegar, plus chopped red and green chiles, and 2 teaspoons each of sesame seeds, sesame oil, and fish sauce.

ukoy
sweet potato fritters
with plantains and shrimp

8 oz. whole, uncooked shrimp
½ cup boiling water or fish stock
I small red bell pepper
2 inches of fresh ginger
I inch of lemon grass or lemon zest
4 scallions, finely sliced
6 oz. sweet potato
8 oz. ripe plantain or green banana
2 eggs
I teaspoon turmeric
I cup rice flour
4 garlic cloves, chopped
2 teaspoons baking powder
peanut oil, for frying
salt and freshly ground black pepper
Makes 24, serves 4–6

Shell the shrimp and set the tail meat aside. Crush the shells well, put in a pan with the water or stock, and simmer, covered, for 5 minutes. Strain into a bowl, pressing through as much flavor as possible. Discard the debris and cool the stock. Seed and core the red bell pepper and cut into ½-inch pieces. Peel the fresh ginger and finely slice it lengthwise. Finely slice the lemon grass crosswise. Cut the sweet potato into ¼-inch cubes. Peel the plantain and cut into small cubes.

Meanwhile beat the eggs and stock into the turmeric, rice flour, garlic, baking powder, salt, and black pepper. Add the red bell pepper, ginger, lemon grass, scallions, plantain, sweet potato, and shrimp meat. Mix quickly together.

Heat about 1 inch peanut oil in a heavy-bottom skillet or wok to 375°F or until a ½-inch cube of bread turns golden brown in about 40 seconds.

Put 4 spoonfuls of the mixture in the hot oil and cook for 50 to 90 seconds on each side, turning over with tongs. Drain on crumpled paper towels and keep hot while you cook the remaining mixture. Serve with the dipping sauces described in the introduction to this recipe.

Mee *krob* is the classic Thai dish that ideally requires a large wok, a pair of tongs, and a ventilator fan. But care, optimism, and an open window will do—and don't try to cook more than one skein of dried vermicelli noodles at a time. Buy the noodles, rice vinegar, fish sauce, *tom yam* stock cubes, and tiny, fiercely hot, birds-eye chiles from an Asian grocer.

crispy thai noodles
with chicken, shrimp, chile, and cilantro

8 oz. fine rice vermicelli noodles

peanut oil, for frying

3 eggs, beaten

7–8 tablespoons superfine sugar

6 tablespoons rice vinegar

4 tablespoons light soy sauce

4 tablespoons Thai fish sauce

½ cup spicy stock, such as stock made from *tom yam* stock cubes

1 tablespoon mild paprika

2 teaspoons coriander seeds, crushed

8 oz. uncooked shrimp, shelled and deveined

4 skinless, boneless chicken breasts, finely sliced

3 cups fresh bean sprouts

6 scallions, sliced lengthwise

3–4 birds-eye chiles, sliced crosswise

1 bunch of fresh cilantro, chopped

Serves 4–6

Separate the layered skeins of noodles without breaking them. Cook one skein at a time. Pour about 2 inches peanut oil into a large wok and heat to 375°F, or until one strand puffs up immediately. Set a large metal strainer over a heatproof bowl. Put crumpled paper towels on a tray, ready for draining the fried noodles.

Using tongs, add a skein of noodles to the very hot oil. Cook for 10 to 15 seconds until puffed up and slightly browned, then turn it over carefully with tongs. Cook the second side, then set it on the paper towels. Repeat until all the noodles have been cooked. If there is any dark debris in the oil, pour all the oil through the strainer into the heatproof bowl, discard the debris, and return the oil to the wok. Reheat and continue cooking the remaining noodles. Pour out the hot oil, return the cooked noodles to the empty wok, and keep them warm.

Heat a small pan, add 1 tablespoon of hot oil, then half the eggs. Cook the omelet briefly on both sides. Remove and repeat with the remaining mixture. Roll up the omelets, slice into strips and set aside.

Wipe out the pan and add the sugar, vinegar, soy and fish sauces, stock, paprika, and cilantro. Heat, stirring, until syrupy. Add the shrimp and poach until firm. Remove and set aside. Cook the chicken in the same way. Increase the heat, add the bean sprouts, scallions, omelet, and shrimp, and toss gently. Tip the mixture over the hot noodles in the large wok. Turn the noodles to coat, breaking them as little as possible. Add the chiles and cilantro, and serve hot.

Rice sticks are dried noodles packed in large skeins. The noodles are about ¼ inch wide, and are a brilliant pantry standby item— very versatile and easy to prepare. Szechuan peppercorns (*Zanthoxylum simulans*) are scented and spicy, rather than hot. They are available from Chinese food stores or specialist spice merchants.

rice sticks
with Szechuan-style sauce

⅔ **cup peanut oil**

½ **cup shelled raw peanuts**

2 teaspoons Szechuan peppercorns

1 small onion, chopped

2 garlic cloves, crushed

1¼ cups freshly made, strong, hot China tea, or green tea

2 tablespoons dark soy sauce

1–2 tablespoons dark sesame oil

2 inches fresh ginger, peeled and finely sliced

2 teaspoons mild paprika

3–4 dried birds-eye chiles, crumbled

juice of 1 lemon

Rice Stick Salad:

8 oz. celery stalks

2 cooked chicken breasts

6 oz. snow peas

8 oz. carrots

6–8 green lettuce leaves

8 oz. dried "rice stick" noodles

1 bunch of fresh cilantro leaves, torn

Serves 4

Heat the oil in a wok to about 375°F, or until a cube of bread browns in 40 seconds. Add the peanuts and Szechuan peppercorns, and cook, stirring, for 1½ minutes. Empty the pan into a metal strainer set over a heatproof bowl. (This prevents the nuts overcooking and scorching.)

Put the contents of the strainer, plus 2 tablespoons of the cooking oil, into a food processor with the onion, garlic, and half the hot tea. Whizz to a paste. Add the remaining tea, soy sauce, sesame oil, ginger, paprika, chiles, and lemon juice, and whizz again to make a sauce.

Remove the leaves from the celery and reserve. Pull the cooked chicken into shreds, or cut into cubes, and finely slice the snow peas, carrots, celery stalks, and lettuce. Put the chicken and vegetables in a pan with some salted boiling water. Cook for 2 minutes, drain and discard the liquid.

Meanwhile, pour boiling water over the noodles and let "cook" for 3 to 4 minutes or until white and firm. Drain. Just before serving, reheat by pouring on some boiling water, then drain quickly and add to the other ingredients.

Put the rice stick noodles in a bowl, add the vegetables, chicken, and sauce, and toss well. Sprinkle with the torn cilantro and celery leaves and serve.

ozoni new year soup
with char-grilled *mochi* rice cakes

There are many versions of this classic celebration soup, but the one constant ingredient is the *mochi* rice cake—a dense, sticky, paste-cake, which even features in Japanese folklore. *Mochi*, like *konbu*, bonito flakes, and daikon, can all be found at Japanese grocers or speciality Asian suppliers. What may be confusing is that there are two kinds available—the soft, freshly made ones, and the hard, dry, pre-packed type. It's the latter you need, which you soak for about 5 to 10 minutes, until softened.

Dashi (stock):
½ oz. konbu (dried kelp)
5 cups cold water
¼ cup sake or rice wine
½ oz. dried bonito flakes
Ozoni:
4 inches daikon (white radish)
I large carrot, trimmed
4 scallions
4 sprigs edible chrysanthemum leaves (shungiku)
12 oz. boneless, skinless chicken breasts, finely sliced
6 uncooked jumbo shrimp tails, deveined
2 inches fresh ginger, finely sliced lengthwise
I teaspoon salt
2–3 tablespoons Japanese light soy sauce (shoyu), or more to taste
4 *mochi* cakes (Japanese dried rice cakes)
Serves 6

1 Heat the *konbu* and water to just below boiling. Remove from the heat and let stand for 5 minutes. Remove the *konbu*. Add the sake and bonito flakes and return to a boil. Simmer 2 minutes, then strain back into the pan.

2 Trim the radish as shown, and slice thinly. Make V-shaped cuts down the length of the carrot and slice thinly. Slice the scallions lengthwise. Tear the chrysanthemum leaves, blanch for 60 seconds, drain, and refresh in cold water.

3 Add the chicken, shrimp, and ginger to the konbu stock. Simmer, covered, for 2 minutes. Add the blanched vegetables to the soup. Add salt and soy sauce, then cover with a lid and simmer gently.

4 To prepare the *mochi* rice cakes, pour near-boiling water over them and set aside for 5 to 10 minutes until softened. Drain, then set aside until ready to broil. Cook under a hot broiler until puffed and golden. Broil the other side.

5 Put one broiled *mochi* cake at the bottom of each soup bowl, then add the soup, taking care to give each bowl a roughly equal share. Serve hot as one course of a celebratory meal.

Go to a Southeast Asian or Chinese supermarket for the various authentic ingredients. Don't be put off by the list—going shopping is half the fun! Cashews, native to Brazil, came to Malaysia with the Portuguese 400 years ago, and are a great alternative if you can't find real candle nuts.

laksa
malay noodle soup

8 oz. dried rice sticks

8 oz. uncooked shrimp

2 cups bean sprouts

1 tablespoon light soy sauce

1¾ cups canned coconut milk

8 oz. ready-made fish balls

4–6 fresh prawns (optional)

½ cucumber

1 large bunch of fresh mint

4 lettuce leaves

Rempah Seasoning:

2 inches fresh galangal or ginger

8 candle nuts, cashews, or macadamias

1–2 dried red chiles

4-inch piece lemon grass

1 tablespoon coriander seeds

4 tablespoons peanut oil

2 garlic cloves, slivered

8 shallots or 2 onions, sliced

2 teaspoons hot paprika

1 tablespoon dried shrimp paste

2 teaspoons ground turmeric

3½ oz. dried shrimp

Serves 4–6

To make the rempah seasoning, slice the galangal or ginger, chop the cashew or candle nuts, seed and chop the chiles, finely slice the lemon grass lengthwise, and crush the coriander seeds. Heat the oil in a small pan, add all the rempah ingredients and stir-fry for 5 minutes.

To make the soup, put the rice stick noodles in a bowl, pour boiling water over them, soak for 5 minutes, then drain them carefully and ladle into 6 small bowls or 1 large serving bowl. Shell and devein the shrimp and put in a large pan with the bean sprouts, soy, coconut milk, fish balls, and prawns, if using. Add 4 cups of boiling water and simmer for 5 minutes.

To prepare the garnishes, cut the cucumber into 2-inch batons, finely slice the lettuce, and tear the mint leaves. Set aside.

Add a ladle of the boiling soup to the pan, then stir the spicy mixture back into the soup and simmer for 6 to 7 minutes. Put the garnishes on top of the noodles in the bowl or bowls. Reheat the pan of soup to near-boiling, stirring to prevent the coconut oil from separating. Ladle the hot broth into the bowls—this will instantly reheat the noodles. Take care to give each bowl a roughly equal share of the solids. Serve hot while all the colors, tastes, and textures remain vivid.

Note: For a main course dish, double the quantity of shrimp, dried shrimp and fish balls, and add an extra 2 cups of water.

These rice flour pancakes are sometimes called "Korean pizzas" by Korean expatriates—they are snack foods often served outdoors, at markets, fairs, and celebrations. In this version I use oysters, but clams or abalone could also be included. Dip the torn or cut portions of the pancakes into the flavorful sauce before eating. Dried Korean chile is sold as either shreds or grains—but you could also use chile powder or crushed chiles.

korean oyster "pizzas"
with chile-sesame dipping sauce

1 lb. fresh oysters, or about 10 oz. canned oysters in brine, or other seafood

¼ cup rice flour

1 cup all-purpose flour

½ teaspoon salt

1 large egg

1 teaspoon dark sesame oil

8–12 scallions

4 tablespoons peanut oil, for sautéing

Chile-sesame Dipping Sauce:

6 tablespoons Japanese soy sauce

4 tablespoons Japanese rice vinegar

2 shallots, finely sliced

1 tablespoon toasted sesame seeds

½ teaspoon chile shreds or grains, crushed chiles, or chile powder

Serves 4

If using fresh oysters, shuck them and reserve the liquid from the shells. If using oysters in brine, drain them and reserve the brine. Make up the liquid to 1 cup with water. (If using smoked oysters in oil, discard the oil.)

Sift the flours and salt into a bowl. Beat in the brine or oyster-water, together with the egg and sesame oil, to form a thin, creamy batter. Let stand while you prepare the other ingredients. Cut the scallions in half crosswise and slice the green parts into diagonal shreds. Cut the white parts lengthwise into quarters.

To prepare the dipping sauce, briefly whizz all the ingredients in a blender. Pour into 4 serving dishes.

Heat 1 tablespoon of the oil in a heavy-bottom skillet or wok, swirling it around to coat well. Toss in a quarter of the oysters and a few bits of scallion. Add a quarter of the batter and some more of the scallions. Cook the pancake 4 to 5 minutes, turn it and cook a further 3 to 4 minutes, until the surface is mottled with brown. Tear into 4 pieces and keep hot, while you cook the remaining pancakes, then serve with small bowls of the chile-sesame dipping sauce.

gói cuôń
ricepaper parcels
with hot and sesame dips

A traditional Vietnamese dish served at communal meals and assembled at the table by the guests. It contains rice in two forms; as **wrappers** (*bañh trang*) and as rice vermicelli **noodles**. Both are sold dry by Asian grocers or larger supermarkets.

This recipe, unusually, includes two **dipping sauces**—a spicy, dry mix and a sweet-sour sauce. Vietnamese mint isn't always available, so you could substitute ordinary garden mint or basil instead.

4 oz. dried rice vermicelli noodles

3½ oz. pork fillet, thinly sliced

7 oz. bacon slices, cut in 32 pieces

32 ricepaper wrappers (*bañh trang*)

16 small uncooked shrimp, shelled, deveined, and halved (about 8 oz.)

2½ cups fresh bean sprouts

16 scallions

8 lettuce leaves, quartered

32 mint or Vietnamese mint leaves

Spicy Chile Dipping Sauce:

2–3 red or green birds-eye chiles, finely sliced

4 tablespoons toasted sesame seeds

4 tablespoons dried coconut

Sweet-sour Dipping Sauce:

3 limes

3 tablespoons fish sauce (*nuoc mam*)

1 tablespoon sugar

2 teaspoons peeled, minced fresh ginger

Makes 32, serves 6–8

1 To "cook" the rice vermicelli noodles, put in a strainer set over a large saucepan. Cover with boiling water and leave for 5 minutes. Drain, rinse in cold water to stop the cooking process, then drain again. Set aside.

2 Place the ingredients for the Spicy Chile Dipping Sauce in a small serving bowl and mix well. To make the Sweet-sour Dipping Sauce, finely slice the lime zest and squeeze the juice. Mix with the other ingredients in a small bowl.

3 Preheat a broiler or stove-top grill pan: cook the pork and bacon on the grill pan for 2 to 3 minutes, or under the broiler on a foil-lined rack, turning the pieces over from time to time until cooked and moist, but not crisp. Set aside.

4 Dip the ricepaper wrappers in hot water, or brush them with the water. Put on a serving platter and cover with a damp cloth. Alternatively, have the guests dip their own wrappers.

5 Pour boiling water over the prepared shrimp. Let stand a few minutes. Rinse in cold water, then drain. Repeat with the bean sprouts. Cut the scallions in half crosswise, then lengthwise, giving 64 pieces.

6 To assemble the rolls, put lettuce on a softened wrapper, add a share of the pork, bacon, shrimp, noodles, mint, bean sprouts, and scallions. Roll up, with the scallion leaves protruding, and serve with the dips.

nasi goreng

indonesian fried rice
with garnishes

Like Cantonese fried rice, *nasi goreng* has traveled all over the world and been adapted along the way. Some Indonesians maintain that it originated in China, but it has always been associated with the *rijsttafel* of Dutch colonial rule. It can combine cooked rice, omelet strips (in this case chile-seasoned as well), vegetables, meat, fish, and aromatics.

Cook the rice 2 to 3 hours ahead. When ready to prepare the fried rice, heat 1 tablespoon of the oil in a skillet and sauté the steak over high heat to seal on both sides—do not cook it fully. Let cool, cut into thin strips, and set aside.

If using dried onion flakes (not the ready-cooked ones) sauté them in 1 tablespoon of the oil until crisply brown. Set aside.

Using a fork, beat the eggs with the chile and salt.

Add 1 tablespoon oil to the skillet, pour in half the egg mixture, adding a little more oil if needed, and make a thin omelet. Turn it over and cook until pale gold on both sides. Make a second omelet with the remaining mixture. Roll up both omelets, slice finely, and set aside.

Put the chopped onions, garlic, and shrimp paste into a food processor and purée to a rough pulp. Heat 2 tablespoons of the remaining oil in a large wok or deep skillet, add the pulp, and sauté for 3–4 minutes until cooked and dry.

Add the remaining 2 tablespoons of oil, the meat, shrimp, cucumber, carrots, and peas or beans. Stir-fry for 2 minutes, then add the rice. Mix well, then sprinkle with soy sauce. Cover and cook briefly to reheat all ingredients, sprinkling in a little water as needed to help create the necessary steam. Sprinkle over the scallions and onion flakes and serve.

1½ lb. cooked white long-grain rice

7 tablespoons peanut oil

12 oz. steak from pork or beef rump

4 tablespoons ready-fried onion flakes (or kalonji)

3 eggs

1 teaspoon dried crushed chile

½ teaspoon salt

2 onions, chopped

3–4 garlic cloves, crushed or finely sliced

1 teaspoon shrimp paste (*blachan*)

8 oz. uncooked shrimp, shelled and deveined

4 inches cucumber, cut into matchsticks

1 carrot, finely sliced and blanched

4 oz. fresh peas or beans, blanched

2 tablespoons light soy sauce

4 scallions, finely sliced lengthwise

Serves 4

japanese sushi

One of the glories of the Japanese kitchen, sushi traditionally involves much ritual, but it is possible to apply the general principles using western utensils. The essentials are Japanese short-grain sushi rice and other authentic ingredients. Japanese grocers stock the rice, *konbu* (kelp), *sushi-su* (rice vinegar), *kurogoma* (black sesame seeds), *umeboshi* (pickled plums), *wasabi* (green horseradish) paste, and *beni-shogu* (pickled ginger). Shown here are three sushi made with two basic methods. Keep refrigerated, then return to room temperature before serving.

2 cups sushi rice, washed and drained
8-inch piece dried kelp (*konbu*)
5 tablespoons Japanese rice vinegar
2 tablespoons sugar
2 teaspoons sea salt
3 inches fresh ginger, finely sliced
3 garlic cloves, crushed
¼ cup Japanese soy sauce
2 oz. Japanese *wasabi* paste
4 oz. pickled pink ginger
Onigiri-zushi (Steps 2–3):
3½ oz. lightly cooked salmon fillet
6 pickled red plums (*umeboshi*)
I sheet dried laver seaweed (*nori*)
Norimaki-zushi (Steps 4–6):
I egg, beaten
I pinch of powdered saffron (optional)
I teaspoon peanut oil
4 sheets dried laver seaweed (*nori*) lightly toasted over a gas flame
2 inches cucumber, cut in 8 thin wedges
¼ red bell pepper, sliced lengthwise
4 scallions, halved lengthwise
Seafood Sushi (Steps 7–8):
6 uncooked shrimp, blanched
6 x ¼ oz. pieces sushi-grade salmon
2 oz. keta or saviar (salmon eggs)
I teaspoon black sesame seeds
6 chives
Serves 6

1 | Put the rice in a pan with the kelp and 2½ cups boiling water. Simmer, covered, for 18 minutes until steam holes appear in the surface. Let stand 5 minutes. Mix the vinegar, sugar, salt, ginger, and garlic, and stir into the rice.

2 | Using wet hands, pinch, squeeze, and pat one-third of the rice into 6 even balls. Push a hole in the center of each. Put some salmon and plum inside. Close the rice and squeeze into shape. Continue this process to make 5 more.

3 | Scissor-cut the *nori* sheet into 12 equal squares or rectangles. Set a piece under and on top of each rice ball. Pat gently to make 6 squares. Put on a serving dish. Divide the remaining rice into 2 parts.

4 | Beat the egg, 1 tablespoon water, and saffron in a bowl with a fork. Heat a skillet, add the oil, then pour in the egg mixture. Cook both sides until set but not browned. Cool, then cut in half.

5 Place 4 sheets of toasted *nori* on 4 sheets of plastic wrap (instead of the traditional bamboo mat). Add a layer of rice to each. Leave 2 plain. Add the omelet, cucumber, bell pepper, and scallions, as shown, to the other 2.

6 Roll up the *nori,* pulling away the plastic as you go. As each roll is complete, wrap in plastic and tie the ends with rubber bands. Cut into 1-inch slices. Remove and discard the plastic. Add the filled *norimaki* to the serving plates.

7 Snip up the belly of each shrimp with scissors. Open out, snip off the shell above the tail, then press flat as shown. Tap the plain slices of sushi roll into rectangles as shown in Step 8.

8 Top the plain sushi with raw salmon, salmon eggs, and shrimp tails. Snip the salmon and shrimp to neaten the edges. Add sesame seeds and chives to the salmon. Serve all the sushi with the soy sauce, *wasabi,* and pink ginger.

Black rice, grown in Thailand, Indonesia, and the Philippines, is actually a dark, garnet red. Pandanus (screwpine) leaf looks like iris and is scented and sweet, but two split vanilla beans can be used instead. If you can't find the suggested tropical fruits, use the prepared fresh red berries shown here.

black coconut rice
with red berries or tropical fruits

2 cups Thai or Indonesian glutinous
"black" rice (actually deep red)
2 pandanus (screwpine) leaves, crushed
and knotted (or 2 slit vanilla beans)
8 oz. coconut sugar, jaggery,
or dark brown sugar
2 oz. coconut powder (sachet)
1¾ cups canned thick coconut milk
Berries or Tropical Fruits:
a selection of fresh red berries, as
shown, or tropical fruits chosen from:
2 bananas, sliced diagonally
2 mangoes, sliced into strips
1 papaya, seeded
4 rambutans (optional)
4 fresh lychees (optional)
fresh banana leaf (optional)
sprigs of mint, to serve (optional)
confectioners sugar, for dusting
(optional)
Serves 4

Put the rice and pandanus (screwpine) leaves (or vanilla beans) in a pan with 4 cups of boiling water and return to a boil. Cover, reduce the heat to low, and cook, undisturbed, for about 25 minutes, or until almost dry.

Remove from the heat and let stand for 10 minutes.

Add the sugar, coconut powder, and a quarter of the coconut milk, and stir until dissolved.

Prepare the berries or bananas, mangoes, and papaya. If using rambutans, cut horizontally around the fruit to expose the white flesh at the center. Pull off and discard the top peel. If using lychees, remove and discard the peel.

To serve, if desired, wash and dry 2 squares of banana leaf and use to line a large serving dish. Overlap the leaves so the 8 points stick up at the edges. Spoon in the still-hot rice.

If not using leaves to serve, simply spoon into a serving dish, or divide the rice between 4 small plates.

Trickle over some of the coconut milk, and serve the rest in a small pitcher. Pile the fruit on top of the rice, add a sprig of mint, and dust with confectioners sugar, if using.

Most Australians and New Zealanders are descended from immigrants from Europe, Southeast Asia, the Far East, the Middle East, and the Americas. Today, their delicious, modern multi-cultural cuisines show influences from all of these culinary forebears.

australia
and new zealand

rice and papaya salad
with banana ribbon crisps and chile-lime dressing

Papaya and mango (shown below) are often used as vegetables in their green, unripe state. Look out for them in Asian greengrocers and even some of the larger supermarkets. Select smoked seafood with a delicate texture: smoked halibut, sturgeon, or eel, hot-smoked mackerel or trout, smoked clams, mussels, or even oysters all work well. Serve this salad, ideally while the rice is fresh-cooked and warm, and the garnishes cold. Choose an interesting sweetening agent for your dressing. Heap up the salads into good high piles. But be relaxed—this is bistrôt fare!

1 cup white easy-cook basmati rice

1 cinnamon stick

Chile-lime Dressing:

1 medium-hot red serrano chile

4 limes

4 tablespoons fish sauce (*nam pla*)

2 tablespoons palm sugar, jaggery,
or light brown sugar

Green Papaya Salad:

2 small or 1 medium-sized green
(unripe) papaya or green mango

1 bunch of fresh cilantro

2 tiny green birds-eye chiles

1 bunch of fresh mint

8 oz. smoked seafood

⅓ cup dry-roasted peanuts, chopped

1 tablespoon pink peppercorns
(optional)

Banana Ribbon Crisps:

1 underripe, green banana, peeled

4–6 tablespoons peanut oil

Serves 4–6

Briefly rinse and drain the rice, and put in a medium-sized pan with the cinnamon stick and a little over twice its volume of boiling water. Return to a boil, reduce the heat to very low, cover the pan, and cook, undisturbed, for 15 to 18 minutes or until all liquid is absorbed, the rice is light and fluffy, and steam holes appear on the surface. Let stand, covered, for 5 minutes.

Seed the chile and slice finely. Finely slice the zest of 1 of the limes, and reserve. Squeeze the juice from all 4 limes, and put in a blender with the fish sauce, sugar, and chile. Whizz to a froth. Stir half the mixture through the hot rice. Remove the cinnamon stick and reserve.

To make the salad, peel the papaya or mango, and remove and discard the papaya seeds. The large mango seed must also be discarded.

Using a food processor, mandoline, or coarse grater, finely slice the papaya or mango. Scissor-snip the cilantro leaves, and finely slice the birds-eye chiles crosswise. Put the cilantro and chiles in a bowl with the mint, seafood, peanuts, and pink peppercorns, if using. Toss with the remaining dressing.

To make the fried banana garnish, use a potato peeler to slice the banana lengthwise into long ribbons. Heat the peanut oil until very hot in a wok or skillet and sauté the banana ribbons until crisp and curly. Drain on paper towels and discard the oil.

Put a mound of dressed rice on each plate, then add the papaya salad, banana ribbons, and reserved zest. Set some fragments of the cinnamon, pulled into pieces, beside the salad.

Note: If the rice must be cooked ahead, microwave it briefly, or steam in a steamer until barely hot. Add its dressing and assemble remaining salad, as above.

These crusty, crunchy cakes of rice with a cheesy, sticky center are a great treat. Add to these some succulent, char-grilled, or plainly broiled fish and a quick-cook pickle of mustard seed, cucumber, and sweet-sharp red chile (almost like jam), and you have a superb, stylish dish for lunch, supper, or a party.

sticky risotto pancakes
with char-grilled fish and chile pickle

2 lb. cooked, chilled risotto (saffron, lemon, or plain) containing at least ½ cup grated Parmesan

⅓ cup polenta, to coat

4 tablespoons extra-virgin olive oil

Char-grilled Fish:

4 boneless fish fillets, such as red mullet, red snapper, gurnard, or trout, about 4 oz. each

4 garlic cloves, crushed to a purée

sea salt and freshly ground pepper

Chile Pickle:

6 tablespoons rice vinegar

3 tablespoons sugar

I teaspoon mustard seeds

I medium hot red chile, seeded and finely sliced

3½ oz. cucumber, unpeeled, finely sliced lengthwise

Serves 4

Divide the cooked risotto into 8 equal portions. Squeeze each one into a ball, then mold into 3-inch round cakes. Pat in polenta to cover.

If using a char-grill, large cast-iron or nonstick skillet, preheat it, then brush with a drizzle of oil. Set all the rice cakes in position at once, and press down towards the end of cooking time, about 7 to 8 minutes. Turn and cook the second side for about the same time.

If using a traditional broiler, preheat first, then cover the rack with foil. Pour half the oil over the foil and put the rice cakes on top. Drizzle with the remaining oil and broil for about 7 to 8 minutes on each side or until pleasantly crusty.

Towards the end of the cooking time prepare the fish: rub some garlic onto each skinless surface. Season well, then add to the broiler pan, char-grill, or skillet. Cook, pressing down firmly, for 2 to 2½ minutes each side. (If using red mullet cook for only about 1¼ to 1½ minutes on each side.)

If using a broiler, cook until flaky, about 2 to 3 minutes on each side, or a little less for red mullet.

To make the pickle, combine all the ingredients in a small saucepan. Stir and boil, uncovered, until the cucumber wilts.

To serve, put the rice cakes on each plate and set the fish on top. Spoon over some pickle and its liquid and serve hot.

Note: 11 oz. raw risotto rice yields 2 lb. cooked weight.

sesame vermicelli
noodles with eggplants and pears

An exotic but easy salad combination, concentrating on textures and exotic tastes. It borrows ingredients from various Asian-Pacific cultures but belongs specifically to no particular one, though it follows classic lines. Many books advise long-soaking noodles in cold water, but I prefer the speedy approach: these vermicelli noodles are virtually cooked by having near-boiling water poured over them.

Preheat the char-grill or broiler. Cut the eggplants into quarters, lengthwise, then cook them first insides towards the heat, then skin sides towards the heat, until charred, soft, and aromatic—about 15 minutes altogether. Cut into ½-inch chunks and set aside.

Put the noodles, star anise, and fungus in a bowl, then pour on boiling water. Let stand for 8 minutes, then drain, reserving 4 tablespoons of the liquid.

To make the dressing put this liquid in a blender with the tahini paste, coconut milk, garlic, soy sauce, and half the sesame oil. Whizz until frothy. Pour over the drained noodles and toss gently to coat. Divide between 4 plates, adding an anise pod and some fungus to each one.

Slice the cucumber and nashi pears into matchstick strips. Toss the eggplants, cucumber, and nashi in the remaining sesame oil and the juice of 2 of the limes, then scissor-snip the parsley and add to the bowl. Spoon the mixture over the noodles, then sprinkle with the black sesame seeds. Cut the remaining lime into wedges and add to the plates.

2 medium eggplants
6 oz. dried rice vermicelli noodles
8 star anise pods
about ½ oz. dried black Chinese fungus
(8 whole or 20–30 pieces)
½ cucumber
2 nashi (Asian) pears
3 limes
1 large bunch flat-leaf parsley
1 teaspoon black sesame seeds, or black
onion seeds (nigella)
Tahini Dressing:
2 tablespoons tahini (roasted sesame
seed) paste
⅔ cup thick coconut milk
4 garlic cloves, crushed
2 tablespoons light soy sauce
2 tablespoons dark sesame oil
Serves 4

Rice in a pie? The idea may seem odd, but this brasserie-style dish is fascinating. A fresh salsa is the second surprise—feijoas are green tropical fruit with a superb, scented taste. They grow well in the Antipodes and are also exported. Kiwifruit taste different, but have similar texture.

rice pie
with a feijoa salsa

5 oz. shortcrust pastry or
pâte brisée, chilled
generous 1 cup white easy-cook
long-grain or basmati easy-cook rice
4 tablespoons sweet chile sauce
1 tablespoon wasabi paste
⅔ cup late-picked riesling, muscatel
or other sweet dessert wine
2 inches fresh ginger, finely sliced
1 teaspoon black onion seeds (nigella)
(optional)
Feijoa Salsa:
4 ripe feijoas or kiwifruit
2 scallions, finely sliced
1 red serrano chile, sliced
2 garlic cloves, crushed
1 large bunch of fresh flat-leaf parsley,
scissor-snipped
2 tablespoons fish sauce (*nam pla*)
2 teaspoons vanilla sugar
2 tablespoons rice vinegar
salad leaves, to serve
Serves 6–8

Roll out the pastry very thinly and use to line a deep, 8-inch pie pan, fluted or plain. Don't worry about untidy edges—they become crisp and can be broken off later. Prick the base with a fork. Line the pie pan with foil and baking beans. Bake towards the top of a preheated oven at 400°F for
15 minutes. Remove the foil and baking beans and cook for a further 10 minutes or until the pastry is golden and crisp.

As soon as the pastry goes into the oven, cook the rice with about twice its volume of boiling water for 15 to 18 minutes, until the water is absorbed, steam holes appear in the top, and the rice is fluffy. Leave the cooked rice to stand for 5 minutes more, covered.

Dissolve the chile sauce and wasabi paste in the wine. Add the ginger, then stir lightly through the rice. Remove the cooked pie shell from the oven and spoon in the seasoned rice—level the surface, but do not pack it heavily. Sprinkle the black onion seeds over the top if using. Let stand.

To make the salsa, cut the feijoas in half crosswise and scoop out the flesh with a teaspoon into a small bowl. Discard the peel. (If using kiwifruit, treat them the same way.) Add the scallions, chile, garlic, parsley, fish sauce, sugar, and vinegar. Taste and adjust the seasonings. Serve warm or cool, but not chilled—on the same day as it is made—in wedges with a dollop of salsa on top and a few salad leaves.

rice varieties

White Long-grain
(Texmati, Carolina, Patna, etc.)
Long-grain, white, milled, not glutinous.
Comments: Mainly savoury use. Absorbs double its volume of liquid. Useful all-purpose rice needing assertive seasoning. Favourite all-purpose and everyday rice in the West. Many varieties available. Cooks with separate grains.
Sources: Grocers, supermarkets, delicatessens.
Cooking and timing: 12–15 minutes or follow package instructions. Cooking methods; pan-of-water, absorption, rice cooker, or microwave.

White Long-grain Easy-cook Rice
(Parboiled long-grain rice)
Yellowish-white (due to extra parboiling processing). Steam-treated (parboiled) then milled. Not glutinous.
Comments: Usually used in savory dishes and as an accompaniment. All-purpose, useful, cooks with separate grains, white and fluffy. It never sticks. More nutritious, because, before milling the grain was parboiled (partially steam treated, which effectively gelatinizes some of the starch.) So more of the B-vitamins are driven deeper into the endosperm or inner part. This means it needs several minutes' extra cooking time. Purists maintain that flavor and aroma are unfavourably affected by the processing. Chefs and caterers prize it for its separate grains. (Note: Italian version is plumper and cooks in 10–12 minutes.)
Sources: Grocers, supermarkets, delicatessens, catering suppliers.
Cooking and timing: 20–25 minutes or follow package instructions. Cooking methods; pan-of-water, absorption, rice cooker, microwave.

Brown Long-grain Rice
(American wholegrain long-grain rice, Texmati, Carolina, Patna, etc.)
Long, slim grain, brown, hulled but not milled. Not glutinous.
Comments: Mainly savory dishes and accompaniments. Absorbs 3–4 times its volume of stock or water. Bulky, filling, substantial. Average cost.
Cooks with a chewy texture, nutty flavor

and is slightly less separate than white. Useful, all-purpose grain, good with distinctive seasonings and flavorings, especially garlic, fresh herbs, and spices.
Sources: Grocers, supermarkets, delicatessens, and wholefood stores.
Cooking and timing: 45–50 minutes or follow package instructions. Takes longer than white rice because it is less refined. Cooking methods; pan-of-water, absorption, pressure cooker, or microwave.

Brown Wholegrain Easy-cook Long-grain
(Brown easy-cook long-grain rice) long-grain, parboiled, unpearled. Golden brown (due to extra parboiling process). Steam-treated (parboiled) but not milled. Not glutinous.
Comments: Mainly savory use. Highly nutritious but harder for some to absorb. Dense, chewy texture, some aroma, and nutty taste. B-vitamins and minerals in good amounts. High in fiber, low in calories. Takes longer to cook than white and non-steam-treated equivalent. Store in a cool, dark place or refrigerate, since natural oils in bran layer can become stale and rancid. Use promptly. Often needs assertive seasoning and flavorings such as garlic, flavored oils, fresh herbs, and spices.
Sources: Wholefood stores, good supermarkets, delicatessens, specialist grocers, wholesalers.
Cooking and timing: About 45–60 minutes (because less refined), or follow package instructions. Cooking methods; pan-of-water, absorption, pressure cooker, or microwave. Chefs and caterers prize it for its separate grains.

Spanish Calasparra
(Paella rice or Bomba, Balilla Sollana)
Round to medium-grain (*Redondo*, in Spanish). White, milled. Not glutinous, but cooks to a slightly sticky but dry state.
Comments: Superb, high quality, robust rice grains: delicious, firm-textured. Calasparra is grown near the Spanish town of the same name in Murcia beside the Seguro and Mundo rivers. Governed by *Denominación de Origen* regulations, it is *Categoria Extra*. Expensive, highly regarded. Best cooked in

large shallow metal *paellera* pans, lidless, with two handles. If Calasparra is difficult to find, substitute Italian risotto rice.
Sources: Spanish grocers, specialist importers, delicatessens, wholefood stores.
Cooking and timing: 15–18 minutes. Paella takes longer since many ingredients and processes are being added while rice cooks and liquid evaporates from uncovered pan. Usually absorbs 3–4 times original volume of liquid. Should cook to quite dry.

Italian Risotto Rice
(*Superfino* grade; Carnaroli, Arborio, Roma, Baldo. *Fino* grade; RB 265, Razza, Vialone, Nano. *Semifino* grade; Ardizzone, Maratello, Ribe, Europa, Loto. *Commune* or lowest grade; Ordinario, Ballila)
Milled, not glutinous. Hard, but cooks to a plump, tender, but al dente state.
Comments: Superb, large, medium to long-grain. White with visible chalky lines or dots in parts. Perfect for soupy, creamy risotto. Grown in the Po Valley in Northern Italy. Rice is the staple in the north, pasta in the south. The higher the quality the more liquid it absorbs—up to 4 times its original volume. Produces a sumptuous, creamy risotto with separate grains. (Most rice types absorb only 2–3 times their own volume.)
Sources: Italian grocers, delicatessens, specialist supermarkets, wholefood stores, specialist importers.
Cooking and timing: Carnaroli and Arborio cook in 18–20 minutes but, because of the 3 or 4 stages of adding the hot liquid, the initial cooking in butter and the regular stirring to check absorption and allow liquids to evaporate, it takes 25–26 minutes in total. (Final cooking in the oven would also add time.)

Italian Pudding Rice
Roundish, short-grains. White, milled. Not glutinous, but sticky and soft.
Comments: Cooked grains cling together and don't keep a definite form. Used for sweet dishes as a thickener, especially custards, molded desserts, and puddings. Mild-flavored, often combined with dairy products such as milk, cream, butter, and eggs. Inexpensive, but can be used to create surprisingly classy dishes. (Heretical fact:

could actually be used for sushi if expensive Japanese sushi rice were unavailable.)
Sources: Grocers, supermarkets, corner stores, delicatessens, wholefood stores.
Cooking and timing: About 15 minutes (though recipes often allow longer to allow for evaporation of liquids, blending of flavors and, in the case of oven cooking, formation of a brown crust or "skin"). 2 oz. of pudding rice can thicken 2½ cups of liquid. Sets to a gel when cold.

Camargue Red Rice
(Griotto rice)
Oval, medium-grain. Brownish-red color, created by a spontaneous mutation, color visible on pericarp. Milled, not hulled. Not glutinous (but cooks slightly sticky).
Comments: Unique strain with a subtle flavor and red color. A premium product, often grown by organic methods. Confined to the wetlands of France's Camargue region. Similar types are indigenous to West Africa (*Oryza glaberrima*), Goa in India, and some parts of the USA. Earthy taste, chewy, firm texture, good appearance. Tipped to be a future culinary "star".
Like wild rice, it suits assertive treatment and seasoning, such as garlic, fresh herbs, and some acidity. Excellent with game, duck, or goose where color can be used to advantage. (Beware of cooking with seafood —the natural rosy pigment dyes the fish.)
Sources: Delicatessens, specialist grocers, specialist supermarkets, wholefood stores.
Cooking and timing: 45–60 minutes or follow package instructions. Cooking methods; pan-of-water, absorption method, pressure cooker, microwave.

Black Glutinous Rice
(Black sweet rice, wild sweet rice)
Short to medium-grain. Actually garnet red, not black. Milled. Red color only in outer layer of milled grain. Glutinous. High in amylopectin. Note: glutinous rice does not contain gluten.
Comments: Rich, earthy flavor. Combines well with coconut sugar, other palm sugars, coconut milk, and pandanus. Usually used in sweet dishes. Not a staple except in Laos, Vietnam, Cambodia, Thailand. Only 2% of world harvest is glutinous (sticky) rice.

Sources: Asian grocers and supermarkets, specialist delicatessens.
Cooking and timing: 25–30 minutes. (Beware: color "dyes" other foods present.) Cooking methods; absorption, additional liquids as needed, rice cooker, or microwave.

White Basmati Rice
(Many types, including Punni, Dehra Dun, Jeera-sali, Delhi, and the golden-hued Golden Sela, and Ambre Mohu)
Long, slim grain with fine, clean scent. White, milled, not glutinous: famously separate, fluffy grains.
Comments: If most people had to choose one rice, this would be it. Grows in the Himalayan foothills and considered by many to be the world's finest rice. Often aged and always treated with respect. Wonderful aroma. Mainly savory, used especially with curries, also in pilaus, pulaos, pollos, pilafs, pullows, where separate grains are wanted. Used in some sweet dishes such as Kheer.
Sources: Indian and Pakistani grocers, good supermarkets, delicatessens, specialist grocers, wholefood stores.
Cooking and timing: 10–12 minutes, or follow package instructions. Amazingly convenient, mostly cooked by absorption method, but also rice cooker or microwave.

White Easy-cook Basmati Rice
As above, technically white but gold tones due to parboiling (steam treatment). Parboiled, then milled. Not glutinous.
Comments: Partially steam-treated to gelatinize some of the starch and drive valuable B-vitamins deep into the grain. Nutritionally superior, but needs several minutes extra cooking time. Each grain remains separate and fluffy. Never sticks. Process first used centuries ago in India, where it forms the staple of the traditional vegetarian diet.
In the West, it is most favored by chefs who prefer each grain to remain separate. In culinary terms it is considered to have a less superb scent and its taste is somewhat altered, making it less desirable to some people. In India, largely nutritional issues dominate in its choice and use.
Sources: Most grocers, supermarkets.
Cooking and timing: 18–20 minutes or

according to package instructions—longer than untreated basmati. Mostly cooked by absorption method, but also by pan-of-water, rice cooker, or microwave.

Brown Basmati Rice
("Unpearled" or "unpolished")
Long, slim grain. Brown, not milled. Only husk removed. Not glutinous.
Comments: Use as basmati rice. Highly nutritious (but harder for some people to absorb). Dense, chewy texture, nutty flavor, fair aroma. High in B-vitamins and fibre but low in calories. Takes longer to cook than white basmati. Store in cool, dark place, or refrigerate since natural oils in the bran can become rancid. Use promptly. Good when well-seasoned: often combined with garlic and fresh herbs.
Sources: Wholefood stores, delicatessens, good supermarkets, specialist grocers.
Cooking and timing: 45–60 minutes because it is less refined. Follow package instructions. Cooking method; usually pan-of-water, but also pressure cooker, or microwave.

Thai Fragrant Rice
(Jasmine rice, sweet rice)
long-grain. White, milled. Slightly sticky (glutinous). Note: glutinous rice does not contain gluten.
Comments: Mainly savory use. The favorite everyday rice of Thai and Southeast Asian cooks, often known as jasmine rice, especially in Vietnamese cooking. Authentic savor for a large range of Southeast Asian dishes. Slight stickiness makes it perfect for Western as well as Eastern palates. Good with Thai-style curries, stir-fries, or in pulaus. Some people rinse cooked rice under boiling water to separate clumps.
Sources: Asian grocers and supermarkets, specialist supermarkets, delicatessens.
Cooking and timing: 12–15 minutes, 25 if cooked in double-boiler, or follow package instructions. Cooking methods; double boiler, absorption, pan-of-water, rice cooker, or microwave.

Japanese Sushi Rice
(Japanese sweet rice, Japanese medium-grain rice, Japanese sticky rice, Korean rice, Kokuho Rose)

Plump, short-grain. White, milled. Glutinous. Note: glutinous rice does not contain gluten.
Comments: Sticky, absorbent, perfect for sushi where grains must stick together. Expensive, high quality, needs less water than other types. Take care to avoid sticking.
Sources: Japanese supermarkets, delicatessens, Asian grocers, specialist supermarkets.
Cooking and timing: 15–20 minutes plus standing time, or follow package instructions. Cooking methods; absorption, rice cooker, or microwave.

Wild Rice (Zizania aquatica)
("Indian" rice, Tuscarora rice)
Very long, glossy grain. Dark brown to purplish-black, husked but not milled. Not glutinous.
Comments: Not a true rice, but an aquatic grass. Once truly wild and merely gathered in a trade mainly controlled by Native Americans. Native to Eastern, Central, and North America. Now cultivated. Delicious, nutty, earthy taste works well with feathered game, poultry, and many kinds of seafood. When fully cooked the grains may "flower," or "butterfly"—one or both ends spring apart to reveal the white interior. Mainly savory use. Expensive, good quality product. Swells to 2½–4 times original volume when cooked.
Sources: Good grocers, wholefood stores, specialist supermarkets, delicatessens.
Cooking and timing: 55–60 minutes, or follow package instructions.

Basmati and Wild Rice Mixed
Long white (basmati) and long brown-black (wild rice) mixture. Not glutinous.
Comments: Mainly savory use. Relatively new "convenience" product, created in Europe, particularly useful because of speed and ease of cooking and relative cheapness (yet both are premium products). The two kinds of rice are separately pre-treated so that their eventual cooking time is equal.
Sources: Good grocers, luxury goods stores, specialist supermarkets, delicatessens, wholefood stores.
Cooking and timing: 20–25 minutes—much quicker than for traditional wild rice. Cooking methods; pan-of-water, absorption, rice cooker, or microwave.

acknowledgments

My thanks go to Fiona Lindsay, Linda Shanks, Jeremy Hopley, Wei Tang, Catherine Rowlands, Fiona Smith, Annabel Hartog, Amanda Hills, Christine Boodle, and all at Ryland Peters & Small and Tilda Rice (especially Lesley Wood).

I also wish to thank the following experts and authors whose works have inspired and so informed me:
Madhur Jaffrey The Flavors of India, Far Eastern Cookery
Bruce Cost Foods from the Far East
Tess Mallos Complete Middle Eastern Cookbook
Charmaine Solomon Oriental Collection
Evan Jones American Food: The Gastronomic Story
Sada Fretz Pilaf, Risotto, and Other Ways with Rice
Heidi Haughy Cusick Soul and Spice
Steven Raichlen Miami Spice
Camellia Panjabi 50 Great Curries of India
Rena Salamon Greek Food
Meera Freeman The Vietnamese Cookbook
Claudia Roden Mediterranean Cookery, A New Book of Middle Eastern Food
Tom Stobart The Cook's Encyclopedia
Vicky Hayward The Grain of Life, Gourmetour
Anna del Conte Classic Food of Northern Italy
Elizabeth Lambert Ortiz Japanese Cookery, The Book of Latin American Cookery
Maria José Sevilla Spain on a Plate
Jean Andrews Red Hot Peppers
Paola Gavin Italian Vegetarian Cookery
Richard Olney (Ed.) Grains, Pasta, and Pulses, Time Life Books
Yamuna Devi Art of Indian Vegetarian Cookery
Sri Owen The Rice Book, Indonesian and Thai Cookery
Dorinda Hafner A Taste of Africa
Leslie Forbes Recipes from the Indian Spice Trail
John Spayde Japanese Cookery
Cheong Liew and Elizabeth Ho My Food
Susanna Foo Chinese Cuisine
Robert Carrier Taste of Morocco
Christopher Idone Brazil: A Cook's Tour
Francis Bissell Sainsbury's Book of Food
Victoria Alexander and Genevieve Harris The Bathers Pavilion

planning rice menus

Soups

Caldo verde soup (Portugal) **38**

Pumpkin chowder with rice and thyme (France) **41**

Ozoni New Year soup with mochi rice cakes (Japan) **110**

Laksa Malay noodle soup (Malaysia) **115**

Appetizers

Red mullet tamales with tomato chile dip (Mexico) **18**

Suppli cheese balls with basil and pignoli nuts (Italy) **37**

Rice and buckwheat blini (Russia) **42**

Greek dolmathes (Greece) **45**

Korean oyster "pizzas" with chile-sesame dipping sauce (Korea) **116**

Ricepaper parcels with hot and sesame dips (Vietnam) **118**

Japanese sushi (Japan) **124**

Rice and papaya salad with banana ribbon crisps and
    chile-lime dressing (Australia) **132**

Rice pie with a feijoa salsa (New Zealand) **139**

Risotto, Noodles, and Fried Rice

Lobster and lemon risotto on a bed of bitter greens (USA) **14**

Saffron risotto (Italy) **51**

Wild mushroom risotto (Italy) **51**

Classic Cantonese fried rice with scallions, ham, and crab (China) **102**

Fried rice with smoked fish (China) **102**

Fried rice with chicken, smoked seafood, and tarragon (China) **102**

Crispy Thai noodles with chicken, shrimp, chile, and cilantro (Thailand) **106**

Rice sticks with Szechuan-style sauce (China) **109**

Nasi goreng Indonesian fried rice with garnishes (Indonesia) **122**

Sesame vermicelli noodles with eggplants and pears (New Zealand) **136**

Fish and Seafood

Pan-fried crab cakes with spicy oriental sauce (USA) **16**

Traditional jambalaya with chorizo and shrimp (USA) **22**

Seared swordfish with wild rice and black bean salsa (USA) **29**

Kedgeree with smoked fish and crème fraîche (Great Britain) **36**

Spanish paella with chicken, shrimp, and squid (Spain) **46**

Tanzanian fish curry with mustard seed rice (Tanzania) **76**

Sticky risotto pancakes with char-grilled fish and chile pickle (Australia) **135**

Poultry

Cajun gumbo with Jerusalem artichokes (USA) **24**

Spicy Camargue rice with char-grilled duck breasts (France) **52**

Chestnut rice stuffing with roasted turkey breast (Greece) **55**

Chicken pulau with almonds, orange, and pistachio (Afghanistan) **64**

Chicken and peanut stew with red dendé rice (Mali) **77**

Chicken korma with pistachio basmati rice (India) **86**

Meat

Rice and peas with Jamaican hot chile sauce (Jamaica) **30**

Lamb and rice sausage with parsley, lime, and spices (Iran) **66**

Lamb biryani with cilantro and cinnamon (India) **88**

Gingered pork chop masala with cashew rice (India) **92**

Vegetables

Stuffed cabbage leaves with sauerkraut and a red
    bell pepper sauce (Germany) **56**

Pearl divers' rice with saffron and honey (Bahrain) **65**

Stuffed vegetables with rice and sour cherries (Iran) **68**

Moroccan couscous with rice, lemon, and tahini (Morocco) **78**

Orange and pumpkin pulao with two cachumbers and a raita (India) **82**

Spicy seeded pilaf with okra and spinach (India) **85**

Sweet potato fritters with plantains and shrimp (Philippines) **105**

Desserts

Honey rice ice cream with orange and saffron (Great Britain) **61**

Almond rice custard with berries or pomegranate seeds (Turkey) **73**

Kheer rice pudding with cardamom and pignoli nuts (Sri Lanka) **95**

Black coconut rice with red berries or tropical fruits (Indonesia) **129**

Cakes and Cookies

Spiced shortbread cookies with rosewater and pistachios (India) **96**

Spicy coconut loaf with cashews and cardamom (India) **98**

index